A [illegible]

M [illegible]

Ordinary

One man's life experiences and the effects of change especially with the UK's EU membership

by

Ken Wight

The June Press

First published in 2016

by The June Press Ltd

UK distributor
The June Press Ltd
PO Box 119, Totnes
Devon TQ9 7WA
Tel: 44(0)8456 120 175
Email: info@junepress.com
Web: www.junepress.com

ISBN 978-0-9927501-2-1

Cover photo - Ken's sisters June and Jill
Backpage photo - Ken's family

Contents

This royal throne of kings, this sceptred isle,
This earth of majesty, this seat of Mars,
This other Eden, demi-paradise,
This fortress built by Nature for herself
Against infection and the hand of war,
This happy breed of men, this little world,
This precious stone set in the silver sea,
Which serves it in the office of a wall
Or as a moat defensive to a house,
Against the envy of less happier lands, --
This blessed plot, this earth, this realm, this England.

William Shakespeare. *"King Richard II", Act 2 scene 1*
Greatest English dramatist & poet (1564 - 1616)

Dedication

In memory of Peter Harcup 1954 - 2015

The very first time I met Peter was in September, 1966, when he and Charlie Appleton walked together, up the steps and, into the playground of William Penn secondary school in Manor Park.

It was the first day of the new school year; I was moving up to the fourth year and we were watching the new intake of first year pupils as they arrived. What I noticed most was the sheer size of Peter 6ft 4inches, and his smiling pleasant face, accompanied by his best friend, Charlie, with his cheeky smile and long hair. They were always together and always cheerful.

We knew most of the new kids and their families because we all lived nearby. Dave Harcup, for example, was in my year, and Eddie, in the year below. I knew most of Charlie's family from Chatfield; his mum 'Blackie', 'Tinny' and Peter and his sisters, and so on. His neighbours, John Clifford and Paul Carpenter were my class mates.

When it was that the Harcup family moved to Belfast Avenue I can't remember exactly but we all became friends, with a few ups and downs. I was born in Belfast Avenue and moved to nearby Waterbeach Road when I was 14.

My younger brother, Jimmy, had a fight with Danny, and for the next two weeks, walked around terrified in case he bumped into one of the older brothers. Luckily, it was Peter that he met with. He walked straight up to Peter and told him what had happened; and it went like this: 'Pete, I'm really sorry, but I've had a fight with Danny, so can you hit me now and get it over with?' and Peter said something like: 'I'll be having words with Danny and I'll sort it with the others'.

Dave was the one I knew the best because he was in my year, and after we left school, he and Monty White used to hang around together. I went around with Mick Carpenter, Allen Deverill, Phil Townsend, Jimmy Hearne, Keith West and Eddie Humphries because we all had motorbikes and used to meet in the Orchard Youth Club.

Eddie Harcup used to come around to Mick's house in Oatlands Drive, and on one occasion turned up with a new record by Barry Ryan, called 'Eloise' that we listened to on the record player, I loved that song and went out and bought it straight away.

I liked Eddie, and knew him from school but we never seemed to hit it off - probably my fault - and I fell foul of him; something I regret to this day. It was about this time that I'd try to avoid Peter, because I was sure that he wouldn't extend the same leniency to me, as he'd shown to my younger brother. What a bloody fool I was!

Well the fateful day came, when I turned into Waterbeach Road, one Saturday afternoon, by Baylis Court School, and there was Peter, walking towards me, in the middle of the road. I swear my heart stopped, but I needn't have worried, because up went his hand and with a beaming smile: 'Kenny; hello Ken. How are you, where are you going, how's the bike?' I think I was in shock and said something like: 'Er, yeah, um, yeah, and great!' and rode around him thinking 'he probably doesn't know yet'.

Anyway, every time we ever met it was always the same greeting. I was amazed at how cheerful and friendly he was all the time.

A year or so later, I had just left my girlfriends house in Upton Lea and was catching the bus by the shops. It was just after 10 o'clock on a Monday night and the bus would be full of teenagers who had been to 'Jessica's' disco in Wexham. Who was the first person I set my eyes on? Well you couldn't miss him; it was Peter, with his girlfriend, later to become his wife. Then there was that great smile again, leaning forward, arm across the bar in front, his big long legs in the aisle, and the same greeting. What a great, marvellous young man.

The last time I saw Peter was in the Bishop Centre in 1986. He was working as a plumber for the council, and when he saw me, he stopped his van and we had a chat; he was joking about as usual, then off he went.

Several years later, I saw Charlie down his yard in Chalvey, and asked him how Peter was . It was then that he told me about Peter's illness; I was shocked; that was so unfair.

Just recently, I was having a particularly difficult few weeks where everything was getting on top of me, but what upset me most was when I saw in the *Observer* that Peter Harcup had passed away peacefully at Wexham Park Hospital. That destroyed me, I was choked up.

Then I continued reading: 'much loved by all his family and friends'. It made me feel happy that it was a peaceful passing surrounded by people who loved this great, gentle man.

God bless you Peter.

Acknowledgement

I met Chris Hoskin during my first general election campaign, in 2005, when I stood for UKIP as parliamentary candidate in Watford. I was amazed by his vigour and enthusiasm. He has supported me enormously with my endeavours, and especially with my book.

As an author in his own right, his help has been invaluable and has guided me through to completion. Thank you Chris.

Life begins

I was born on the 8th September 1951 but my earliest memories only go back as far as to when I was a child in a cot. I can't remember if I could walk or talk then, but when I was standing in my cot my head was level with the top bar, so I imagine that I was about a year to eighteen months old. I was aware of everything that was going on around me at that time and this memory is still very vivid in my mind today. I was one of seven children, having five older sisters and a younger brother. Whilst in my cot I remember seeing adults and older children, but I don't remember seeing any babies which meant that my younger brother hadn't been born yet.

My younger brother Jim is two years younger than me so that would confirm my age at that time. I can remember that the cot was downstairs against the back wall next to the door of the kitchen, in the front room of the house that I grew up in; it was early in the morning, as my mum was getting dressed and having breakfast at the same time. There was another woman there helping and I suspect that it was my older sister. After a short while there was a knock on the door and in came a smartly dressed young woman looking very official but with a kind smiling face who I later found out to be Miss Boroughs, our welfare officer, who dressed in tweed, wore brown leather shoes and drove a Morris Minor 1000. We all went in her car to William Penn nursery where I was left; this happened frequently but not long term because I remember being with my mother all the time, always visiting friends, aunts, uncles and grandparents.

There was no television in our house, it was dark and brown with bare floorboards but with a cheery open coal fire. I loved being with my mum and was very happy.

In some of the rooms, the bottom half of the walls were painted dark green and the top half in cream; it was only when I was around nine years old that a council inspector came and told us they were going to decorate any three rooms with wallpaper. So we opted for the living room, the main bedroom and the staircase as did most of our neighbours.

The next thing I remember very clearly was being put to bed in a very nice but unfamiliar room where there was a double bed by the side of my cot, and on the far side another, painted tubular steel, identical cot with a small child in it who looked younger, but not new born. It was my brother, but I don't remember seeing him before this.

The next day at breakfast we were sat in highchairs at a long wooden table, and around it sat twenty or so other mothers and their children. There were other women there in nurses' uniforms looking after the mothers, but this wasn't a hospital. It was a very happy and friendly atmosphere. As we finished our breakfast the room began to clear and three or four nurses came over and began to make a fuss of us and told us that our Dad was coming to visit us today; everyone seemed very happy.

When Dad arrived we all walked outside, it was a beautiful warm day and the sun was shining. From the outside we could see that the house was large and stood in its own grounds surrounded by a high wall. The grounds were vast; there were no other houses just lots of trees and countryside and a garden that went on forever. There were several other people about us, walking, talking and relaxing in the sunshine; it was all very peaceful and calm. I later discovered that this place was a convalescence home in Bexhill-on-Sea.

On one or two occasions when I was quite young, all of us children were placed in short-term foster homes, which I found particularly distressing, but the families that we stayed with were extremely kind and looked after us very well. The fond memories I have of that time are still very vivid, and remain with me to this day.

On one of those memorable occasions we were placed with Mr and Mrs Godbold who had two children of their own; a boy of 6 and a girl of 12, the same age as me and my sister, respectively. My other sisters stayed with another family a few doors along, so we were pretty much all kept together. My brother, who would have been 4 years old, stayed with my mum. Jim and Cynthia Godbold were a typical, respectable working class family who lived in a modern 1950's built council house in Morris Close, Langley. I say modern because it was so different to the house that I lived in, which was built in the 1930's, and that wasn't all.

From the minute we walked in the front door with our welfare officer, Miss Burroughs, I noticed that it was fully carpeted, there was a three-piece-suite, it was nicely decorated and had full-length curtains on a rail that opened and closed by pulling a cord, but most amazingly, there was a telly in the corner, at which Jim, in full moustache and slippers, sat opposite smoking a pipe by the fireside, watching the football results and marking his coupon. Mrs Godbold, who opened the door, led us through to the kitchen which was light and bright, and pleasantly painted in yellow and white, with Marley tiles on the floor.

We were given our own carpeted bedroom with spotless bed linen and crisp white sheets. Regular meal times were observed, which was new to me. I for example, was told to always put my sandwich back on the plate after taking a bite and to keep my mouth closed whilst eating, something I continue to do to this day. How about being gently coaxed to eat lettuce (which I thought was raw cabbage) with a sprinkling of salt? Very tasty! Or seeing a suet pudding being boiled in a sack? But that spotted-dick was the best thing I'd ever tasted.

There was a choice of cereals, or toasted soldiers and boiled eggs for breakfast and cooked meals at tea time, with supper before bedtime; which was usually a cup of cocoa and a biscuit. Pure delight! I'd never experienced anything like it. In our house, the cupboard was always bare, except for what my mum called the 'basics', which was milk, bread, half a pound of Stork margarine, 2lb sugar and occasionally a jar of jam, the jars of which were recycled and used as drinks mugs.

In the morning Jim would put on his mackintosh, a cork peaked crash helmet, the sort you see in 'Heartbeat', collect his moped from the back shed and walk it through the alley, across the green and onto the road before starting it and going off to work. Mrs Godbold would get the children off to school, put on her pinafore apron 'piny' and set about the chores, cleaning, shopping and cooking. Being only six years old it was decided that I should stay at home with 'mother' that was great fun because I suppose that I got spoilt. I remember thinking that this was the sort of place I could get used to; everything was so perfect.

Infant life

My next memory is of being very young and being totally reliant on my mum; following her around the house holding onto her apron strings, until one day Miss Burroughs arrived in her Morris Minor and took us around to Godolphin Infants School to meet the teachers. I was given a small bottle of milk and taken to class where I met other children of my age, some of whom I recognised from nursery. We did activities and then listened to stories from a large wooden speaker that always began with some chimes and a woman's voice that said: 'are you sitting comfortably? Then we shall begin'. After a while we heard a hand bell being rung in the corridor for dinner time; we all stood up and were taken to the dinner-hall where we had a hot meal followed by pudding. I thoroughly enjoyed my delightful time at Infants. When you're young you don't have much concept of time. A year for example is a big chunk of your life, but I remember being around six or seven when we were taken across the playground, which was divided in two by a 4ft high wooden fence with a gate (attached to which, was a flag pole, flying a full sized Union Jack) to separate the Boys from the Girls, to look at the Junior school in the building opposite. We had to form a line and walk in pairs; I was with my friend Joey Gieble who was bigger than me and wore national health glasses with a piece of brown paper covering one eye. I felt sorry for him, because he and his younger brother lived in a home nearby called Manor Lodge and slept in a dormitory with a couple of dozen other kids; I don't think he saw his parents much, if at all. I think where he lived might have been an orphanage. In my class we also had a Rudolph Koch and a Paul Weisler; were they German? If they were, you couldn't tell because they spoke perfect English with a local accent.

For the first time I remember being aware that this year was called 1958 and that soon a new year would start after midnight, but crucially, it was tradition that the first person to cross the threshold should be a dark-haired male; or failing that, anyone carrying a piece of coal had to come in the front door, walk through the house then out the back door. This ritual officially brings the New Year in and takes the old year out. At the stroke of midnight all the neighbours would open their doors and ring bells and Mr Henderson next door would dress in a kilt and play 'Auld Lang Syne' on the bagpipes. At only seven years old, and one of seven children, I was enjoying the comfort of routine, and being surrounded by my mum, five older sisters and my younger brother Jimmy. My Dad was only there occasionally and I probably only saw him half a dozen times all the while I was growing up, until I met him again when I was nineteen.

We were only allowed in the garden at that age so everything that happened in the street was an event, and by those events, I mean street-traders. There was no aircraft noise except for one or two propeller driven commercial flights, leaving London airport as it was then called, not like the constant roar of jet engines every two minutes that we get today. So when we heard a noise we would be at the fence taking a look, and it would turn out to be the Coal-man or the Rag-and-Bone cart calling at the top of their voices, but we could never make out what they were saying just that they had their own distinctive recognisable call. What baffled me most was how those men, and they didn't look that big, could carry on their backs a hundredweight (50kg) sack of coal, almost as big and as heavy as themselves; sometimes a dozen at a time into one house? I think that everyone burned coal in the 1950's because the coal lorry was a common sight, and the fact that there was plenty of coal yards in and around Slough. An unpleasant consequence of burning that amount coal on open fires was of the dire air pollution commonly manifesting itself as thick fog. Coal fires are very nice to have, but are high maintenance and wastefully inefficient, and of course they only heat one room. In the middle of winter the bedrooms would be extremely cold and ice would form on the inside of the windows, because don't forget, there was no double-glazing or loft-insulation so the temperature inside was probably close to the temperature outside. There were fireplaces in two of the bedrooms, so at bedtime my mum would take a few shovels full of hot coals from the main fireplace, and put them into the grates upstairs to warm the rooms. Additionally, a brick heated up in the fire, and wrapped in newspaper was a good bed-warmer.

Tradesmen came down our street every day of the week except on Sundays which was reserved for the local vicar making house calls. It made for a very interesting time to see all these people coming and going especially in the school holidays. There was the Dry-cleaners van, a man delivering tar-covered logs, the Bakers-van, the Greengrocers van, the 'Corona' van and the Milk-float which sometimes brought a third of a pint bottles of the best orange juice I have ever tasted. There was the club man, the rent man, the man from the 'Pru', the window cleaner, a man on a three wheeled bicycle sharpening knives, council workers painting, cutting the grass, repairing leaky taps; men from the Gas and Electricity Board emptying the money from the meters, all on foot or by bicycle.

Another trade that I thought was quite tough was that of Dustmen who had to carry the bins on their shoulders from the back gardens to the dustcart and tip the very smelly contents manually; very hard and dirty work then, before wheelie-bins and recycling! There was though, the 'pig bin' in the days when we had swill pigs, that was optional, which was a separate bin for food waste (swill), that the 'pig man' picked up separately. The bin collections were always early in the morning, but nowadays they come at any time; sometimes as late as teatime. That goes for the postman as well.

Once there were two deliveries a day, the first being well before 8am, and the second around midmorning; now the post can arrive anytime, if at all. If the postman becomes so overwhelmed because of manpower shortages, the post just stays on the van until the next day. The demise of the post office is being brought about by the EU's postal services directive 97/67 EC forcing it to open itself to cross-border competition; the outcome being that private companies bid for the most profitable parts, causing the least profitable to be closed down unless we pay far higher costs for the same service. It has been said that essential services should remain in the public domain, and not run as private businesses to make a profit. It's true that they require a small subsidy of £160m/year, but that's small change compared to the £55m a day we hand over to Brussels just for our EU membership. Incidentally, over 3,500 post offices have closed since 1997.

The best sound though, was that of the bell on the Ice-cream man's tricycle, where, if we were lucky, and mum could afford it, we could buy a 'threepenny wafer'.

Across the field were what we called, the field shops; a typical 1950's parade of shops where you could pretty much buy everything that you needed. The first shop was 'Claytons' the grocer, who lived on their shop premises, as indeed most proprietors did in those days, where I would take the order for my mum (when I was a little older) which would be put together in a cardboard box by Mr Clayton (Gilbert) an elderly gentleman who always wore a brown overall type coat, and his wife, a kindly grey haired lady in an apron. That would then be delivered on a Saturday morning by the shop boy on his trade bike along with the bill, which was usually around £2 and ten shillings.

Their shop was basic and spotless and their home, and any time he would see me there on an errand it would be 'hello young master Ken Esquire'. Memorable things that I recall about Claytons were the sweep fan high up on the ceiling, the bacon slicer, a cheese cutting block with wire garrotte, and paper carrier bags with string handles that always used to break. If we ran out of potatoes I would often have to go there for a 5lb bag of King Edwards for Half a Crown (2/6d). Because people had to make their hard earned cash go a long way most people grew their own vegetables and kept chickens for the eggs. It wasn't long after the war and we were still on ration books, times were hard but it brought out the best in people, they were prepared to work hard to improve their standard of living; unlike the state dependency of today that encourages the benefit culture as a career choice.

It was rare to see someone out of work because everyone had to have a job to get by; they worked all week and would usually do their main shopping on a Saturday. Shop workers who worked on a Saturday had time off in the week, and on a Wednesday half day closing all the shops were closed. Sunday was the day of rest and the streets were deserted except for Church goers in their Sunday best. Traditionally the man of the house would go to the local pub between 12 noon and 2pm, also in Sunday best, while the housewife cooked Sunday dinner. Licensing laws were strictly adhered to, there was no 24hr drinking then; pubs closed at 10pm in the week, and 10.30pm on Friday and Saturday.

Because almost everyone observed Sunday as the day of rest I could never figure out why the Off-licence opened at 7 – 10pm and was always busy with parents and kids buying pop and crisps (only plain crisps with a separate blue bag of salt) as a treat. Most families were large then, it wasn't unusual to see 6 children to a family; what is now referred to as the 'baby boom'. My mum couldn't afford it every week but now and then she would treat us to a bottle of Tizer 4 bags of crisps and 2 packets of Cheeselets shared between us all, and it was a real treat to sit around my mum's chair by the fire while she sang to us; her favourites were 'Who's sorry now' and 'You were only fooling' by Connie Francis, and she'd always cry. But the song she found the most poignant was "Happy days and lonely nights'.

With the parting of the ways, you took all my happy days,
and left me lonely nights.
Morning never comes too soon; I can face the afternoon,
but, oh, those lonely nights.
I feel your arms around me, your kisses linger yet,
You taught me how to love you,
Now teach to forget.
You broke my heart a million ways, when you took my happy days,
And left me lonely nights.

1959 was election year so a new trade vehicle appeared on the street. This was different though, inside were two smartly dressed men in suits; one driving, the other talking into a microphone. The message was very loud and clear this time, asking us to vote for someone or other. This would happen two or three times for about a week followed by smartly dressed people handing out posters to go in the windows which said; VOTE for, then the name and picture of the particular candidate that you were in favour of. Being working class council tenants we, of course, always had the red labour poster. I didn't understand the implications of this only that my mum said "we are labour" and naively, I preferred the colour anyway.

Living in a council house had its benefits, and of course working class people could never afford to own their own house even if they wanted to, but they could still have a nice house and live within their means with no extra costs for maintenance and repairs. Each council had a local yard from which all the workmen came when needed. All that was necessary, if you needed a lock changing, had a dripping tap or needed a new draining board was for the tenant to walk to the office, fill out a card and a tradesman was sent out on his trade bike the same week. Simple! If it was a larger job, like changing a bath, repairing fences and gates or something like that, an inspector was sent out from the Town hall. On foot! To me it seems that this was a very cost effective and efficient system; no need for motor vehicles to run and maintain, everything was localised and within walking distance, so there were fewer overheads.

Sometime in the 1970's a central depot replaced the local yards, the workmen then became motorised to enable them to cover larger districts and the waiting lists grew longer and no longer efficient. My sister, for example, in the 1980's, had an old type cast iron overhead toilet cistern that wouldn't flush properly. Now instead of simply walking to a local yard, the tenant had to phone the town hall to get the job done. Anyway, after several phone calls and many weeks later, a plumber in a yellow council van turns up to look at the job, after about half an hour another yellow van arrives, then a while later, another. So in the end there were three workmen crammed into the toilet drinking tea and having a good social!

The conclusion to this jolly fiasco was that the old cast-iron cistern, which was beyond repair, should be replaced with a new one, that another job request needed to be submitted, and that we would be notified. So to sum up then; due to council waste and incompetence, in the name of modernisation to improve efficiency and reduce costs, the savings were: three separate vehicles each containing a driver/operator, each of which without a bloody clue of what they were doing of, about four or five wasted hours and the job completed approximately three months later.

Today there is more money about but people are still struggling.

Money is squandered on fat cats and Quangos, and it appears that there are more (highly paid) Chiefs than Indians, and that is why council tax bills are so high.

There are rich and poor; people who live in big houses and others who dwell in caravans; there are academics and manual workers and so on, and so on. Slough had a good cross section of society living alongside each other. The central part, Manor Park, where I lived was mainly built around the trading estate in the 1930's. Then after the war, building continued into the 1950's, with the huge estates like: the Britwell, Wexham and Langley where, incidentally, the Hawker Hurricane was built, in a factory which later became Fords.

Slough had a good balance of private and council houses with opportunities for all. In school we were constantly told that we could better ourselves by getting a trade, but there was work for all abilities; the council had an army of road sweepers that used to go out every day with their hand carts, that needed constantly replenishing, and factories needed hundreds of people for their production lines. I personally decided at a very early age that I wanted to be an electrician and buy my own house, but not everyone wanted to continue learning by going on to college. They wanted to leave school as soon as possible and get into a job, get married and then onto the council housing list, and I know plenty of people who did just that.

The system in place then could accommodate everyone, but as more and more people flooded into the town, housing became scarce and the waiting list became longer. This was exacerbated by the sale of council houses. Tenants were given attractive discounts to encourage them to buy their own council houses but many weren't suited to home ownership, and consequently, got in over their heads, and struggled with the repayments and the upkeep. These houses were then sold on to the private market leaving a shortage in the council rental sector; in my view, it was all a big mistake from the start.

There is, and always will be a huge demand for council houses, and I maintain that it is the council's responsibility to provide them, keep them nicely painted and decorated, and in a good state of repair. They should make sure that the residents abide by the rules of their tenancy, and strictly enforce zero tolerance for anti social behaviour or 'problem families' as they were previously called, who, incidentally, were few and far between; and this they used to do. They wouldn't tolerate dogs barking, loud music, disruptive or noisy families or commercial vehicles, which all sounds a bit severe, but not overbearing.

People were encouraged to keep chickens and grow vegetables in their gardens, but were not allowed to take down fences or make any alterations inside or out. It was a good system that worked; it was fair and conducive to happy and comfortable neighbourhoods. If you didn't like it, you could always do what I did, and buy your own house. If they really wanted to help people onto the property ladder, why not offer them a lump sum to give up their council houses, they could then buy a new house in an area of their choice, as all potential owner occupiers do, freeing up valuable properties for those on the waiting list.

Why a tried and tested scheme which was backed up by a robust criminal justice system was changed I don't know. Perhaps councils thought that the service had become too much of a liability, and that they could reduce costs by selling off some of their assets to fill their coffers, enabling them to increase bureaucracy and 'fat-cat' salaries, while increasing council tax and closing local amenities such as libraries, swimming pools, schools and playing fields etc, etc; and there lies the problem, top-down government!

None of my friends had phones, we made all our calls from a public call box; heaven knows who we called! But I do remember that, when calling the operator, directory enquiries or 999, the calls were answered after no more than three rings. Automated answering services and queuing were unheard of, it was all about courtesy and loyalty to the customer and providing a good all round service. In other words; Professionalism! All the red phone boxes were the property of the Post Office Telephones and the responsibility of the General Post Office (GPO) and were immaculately maintained. They were cleaned regularly, had a vanity mirror and local dialling codes with instructions, mounted separately, in chrome surrounded glass frames, and contained several directories.

I can't speak for all call boxes, but the one in our street had a light switch under the phone for the convenience of the caller after dark and assumed that the engineer or Policeman switched it off in the early hours. Before the issue of the two-way radio, the Beat Bobby had a whistle, for emergencies and access to the Blue Police Box which contained a telephone linked directly to the Police Station. Members of the public could also use the Box in an emergency. If the station needed to contact a police patrolman at any time, the blue light on the top would flash to alert the officer, therefore, maintaining a direct link to his superiors. Simple and effective, eh! The AA and the RAC similarly, had their own call boxes in their specific liveries for members only, in distress.

On occasions, if a police car were to be required in an emergency, it would pass at considerable speed sounding its twin bells on the front bumper to alert motorists and pedestrians in its path, and that would apply to fire engines as well as ambulances. Thankfully, we didn't have to put up with the constant, multi-tone sirens, which can be heard these days from one side of town to the other, blaring out day and night. Back then it was much more distinguished and civilized.

From the early 1960's things started to go wrong. It was the talk of the street when it was found that someone had broken a pane of glass in our call box. The neighbours were mystified as to who could be responsible; it couldn't be a normal person or someone from our area could it? The vandalism escalated! From tearing pages out of the directories, and damaging the receiver to forcing open the money box and graffiti. This marked the beginning of the demise of the traditional red phone boxes.

*

My passion for double-decker buses started from when it was our main mode of motorised travel either to or from the town, or visiting relations. It was on a cold wet day that we were returning home from town, when my mum surprised us by saying that we were going to take the bus. I wondered why there was this sudden urge to be extravagant, because we had always walked, but I didn't complain because this was going to be a treat. There were lots of people at the bus stop and we weren't able to get on, at least, the first two buses, but they were pretty frequent so it wasn't a real problem. The conductor would supervise the alighting and loading of the passengers. He would call out from the rear platform: 'move along the bus please!' 'room for two more upstairs!'; ring the bell, and as the bus moved off, would reassure those still waiting that another bus would be along shortly, and it would be.

When we climbed aboard the next bus there were only two or three spare seats inside (downstairs) so we had those. My brother and I were only small, so we must have been quite young, and this was the first time that I had been on a bus. It was very exiting! Don't forget, this was a time when kids waved at Steam engine drivers, and they waved back, and we called everyone Sir! We climbed up onto the open platform, then one more step into the bus, helped on by the conductor. Once we were seated, the conductor called out: 'hold tight please!' then rang the bell twice to signal to the driver to move off.

When you get a chance to see an old double-decker, look at the platform, and next to the luggage compartment you'll see a sort of sentry-box; this is where the conductor stands, it's his bolt-hole and where he goes so as not to impede the passengers.

As a kid everything is a new experience so that first bus ride remains vivid in my mind: all the people in their hats and coats, with their umbrellas and shopping (any large or bulky items were placed under the stairs); the warmth, the distinctive smell of the inside of a bus; the small 'golf ball sized' light bulbs, the seating upholstery, the two opposing bench type seats just inside (always my favourite place to sit especially in the summer). It was like a magic place! Everything from the little wind-down windows, the non-slip flooring, the metal domed covers over the wheels and gearbox along the aisle, to the driver up the front, isolated from the passengers in his half-cab (that was another great place to sit). If on further occasions we were waiting for a bus at the station, we'd watch our driver climb up the outside steps to pass though a very small sliding door to get into his seat.

The steering wheel was almost the width of the cab and there were lots of switches above his head and a round indicator disc that used to flash when he turned it to move off. It was absolutely amazing to watch him manoeuvre this huge vehicle effortlessly! Finally the unforgettable sound of the massive diesel engine and the whirring of the gearbox as the bus pulled away. All of this imprinted in my mind in just a few minutes! Once in motion the conductor would collect the fares from his new passengers, and then call out: 'any more fares please! We would then sit quietly and enjoy the ride until our stop, which, along with every other, was always announced in advance by the conductor, who then rang the bell once to stop the bus. PURE MAGIC!

How different it has now all become! Shabby, unregulated buses of all shapes and sizes go along half empty, with masses of cars to contend with all day long. When I was young, the only time there were traffic queues were during rush hours; these times it has become 'rush all hours' except for the wee hours in the morning when people are asleep. I've always maintained that there are some people who are not suited to driving and you yourself probably know one or two.

In the early 1970's I, unbelievably now, knew people who wouldn't drive their cars in bad weather, preferring to cycle to work instead! I for one would much rather go to college by bus, and meet all my friends on the way, even though I, at the time, was one of those rare youngsters who drove, and because I worked hard rewiring houses on the weekends, was able to have a nice car. I preferred big 'six cylinders', like the Ford Zodiac, Vauxhall Cresta, and later the Triumph 2000TC, but these days I don't enjoy driving much at all due to constant all day traffic. Did you know that the South East is second only to Paris for congestion? It's crazy!

In the early 1970's I started to notice the delays, with the appearance of traffic lights at almost every crossroad, and then, maddeningly, on one of the county's largest roundabouts, in the town centre; boasting five sets of lights. On that stretch of road, including the roundabout, that crosses the High Street (A4) from North to South there are 14 sets of lights where there used to be only 3. Even as I write, that junction is being redeveloped into an almost un-navigable multi-lane 'runway' where the traffic refuses to flow. The council, as part of their regeneration scheme call it 'the Gateway to Slough' or should that be the 'Gateway to Hell' to coin the phrase used by Chris Rea when he sang about the M25 being the 'Road to Hell'.

There are cars parked with two wheels up on both sides of the road, in cycle lanes and on grass verges everywhere. If and when there is an accident on the M4 it causes gridlock in towns, villages and inter-connecting roads for miles. There really are too many cars on the roads now; where will it all end?

*

I've always had a passion for motorbikes and still have, but I must admit, a preference for old British bikes. The age of the leather boys, was in the late 1950's and two of my sisters had boyfriends who were 'Rockers'. They would date their boyfriends in places like 'the Cellar' in Windsor, Barton's café (Eddies) on the Bath Road, the Ace café on the north circular with weekend runs to the coast. This was the golden age of the motorcycle, especially the 'café racer' and the 'ton-up' boys; the road bikes were becoming more powerful and much faster and the young boys would customise them with 'clip-ons', rear-sets, swept back pipes etc. to mimic racing machines of the day.

Triumph's and BSA's were the leading makes with the iconic machines being the Bonneville and the Gold Star respectively. Unfortunately, there were many deaths and serious accidents amongst the ton-up boys, probably as a result of high powered machines, inexperienced young men, and no national speed limit. Because of my sister's boyfriends, 'Rockers' on their bikes were regular visitors at our house; well it was an absolute dream for me; we'd wear their crash helmets and goggles (not compulsory then, but part of their outfit) and sit on their bikes, pretending to have a burn-up. Unfortunately, this pretence, in real life had severe consequences. Kenny Budd, the boy next door but one had a pile up on his 'Goldie' which left him a cripple, never to ride a bike again, but he got off lightly compared to some of the other boys. Among the group of boys that used to come to our house, was a big lad they used to call Jumbo; he was killed on the A4 in Langley at the junction by Saint Bernard's Convent. Then there was Bob Wilkinson who owned a motorcycle shop over the field shops. His teenage son and pillion, Alan Lacy were killed together in a single accident. Very sad! I'd see him working at his shop, tinkering with bikes outside with his customers and from a distance with a lump in my throat, wondering how he managed to continue; carrying all that grief, but just getting on with his job. I know the neighbourhood were in shock and grieving at the loss of two young lives.

Before I was born, and when my mum was still living in the East end of London, her two brothers; Jackie 29 and Freddie 23 were both killed in a similar accident on their way to work in Chingford Essex. They were travelling on a road out of town early in the morning when they were in a head on collision with a sand lorry coming over a hump back bridge; the police called at the house and told my granddad that they were found in the ditch by the side of the road and were killed outright. My granddad went totally grey within a week. This was one of the reasons why my mum didn't want her sons to have motor bikes, but did I listen? I loved bikes and had several, and at the age of 17 when I passed my test I had the best bike ever; a Triumph 500cc twin 'Tiger 100'. One can only imagine now how my poor mum must have felt.

Not all the neighbours were nice, some, not many, looked down upon a woman on her own with children; it was frowned upon, and they did try to give us a bad time, but fortunately, the good outweighed the bad.

The cause of many of our problems was our Dad, who probably thought he was smart to drink away all his wages in the pub with his mates, while my mum sat at home waiting with seven children for the housekeeping that never came. Instead, came the drunken beatings, for her daring to suggest that he take responsibility for supporting his wife and family. The problem with my mum, was that she loved him and took the wedding vows seriously, continuing to put up with the abuse and cruelty for far too long, until it finally began to affect her health, when she humbly petitioned for divorce on the 14th November 1956. Thereafter she set about bringing up her children, aged between 3 and 15 years old, on her own.

I'm not saying that bringing up children is easy, in fact I find it quite difficult at times, especially as a single parent; an occupation I wouldn't recommend to anyone. But more importantly, I believe that a child needs the emotional and loving balance that only both parents can provide. I try to make up for that by making sure that my son keeps in touch with the family, and by telling him how special he is. For example, I tell him a story about how when I was out walking, I'd look up and see a large, bright star in the sky; and that the day he was born, that star disappeared; which reminds me of a song by Jim Reeves, "A fallen star'.

A star fell from heaven, right into my arms,
A brighter star I know I've never seen.
Then I found out that it was only you
And all your charms,
Who came into my life to fill a dream.

There were also, of course, plenty of other poor families worse off than us who weren't bad people, just victims of circumstances. Several years later, whilst in the parents' house of my girlfriend, we awaited the arrival of her sister's future in-laws who were coming to visit. The woman spoke to me saying that she had lived in our street when we were young and had gone to school with my sisters but wasn't allowed to play with them as she was warned by her mother not to mix with the 'Scruffy Wights' I told her that I was one of the 'Scruffy Wights' through no fault of our own but because we had a father that didn't support us. To which she replied: 'Oh! I didn't mean you, because you've done well for yourself. She said all this whilst her husband, from whom she had recently become separated because of his infidelity, sat in another corner of the room playing happy families, and boy was she angry! How the mighty tumble! My mum would have said: 'hell hath no fury like a woman scorned'.

The welfare state was still in its infancy in the 1950's and I think worked very well. It provided my mum with a subsistence allowance. A welfare officer would often turn up unannounced to check on us, you know, to make sure that we really were in need of national-assistance and woe betide anyone who broke the rules. It happened to us one day, like this: quite often a kindly neighbour would buy us Easter eggs or give us sweets. It was during a hot summer's day when we were playing outside that our next door neighbour Cathy Henderson treated us to ice creams from the ice-cream van that came down the street.

Can you imagine the scene? There we were all tucking-in when the welfare officer turned up; she charged into the house, started shouting at my mum, and then ran up the stairs to look in the bedrooms to see if anyone was up there that shouldn't be. She then began to lecture my mum on the benefits of welfare and that any money was to be used for absolute necessities and not on luxuries! In addition, the welfare provided our clothing. What happened was, my mum would have to literally go to their office in Slough with the begging bowl. We were then given an appointment to visit the Women's Voluntary Service (WVS) in the High Street.

It was a building called 'Lancaster Terrace' between the Leopold Institute/Slough Public Hall and the General Post Office; there was a doorway on the High Street between the buildings that led to a long staircase to a first floor room where we waited to be seen. All of those grand Victorian buildings were demolished to make way for the new shopping centre. And incidentally, there's nothing there now, just what they call the 'Town Square' it's disgraceful! It's an empty paved area, done on the cheap, where all the dust and 'take-away' wrappers and cartons blow around all over the place like billy-o.

Anyway, back in the WVS, we'd wait to be seen. There was only ever one person there, who would come from an upper floor to ask my mum what we needed; she would then go back up the stairs and into another room then reappear with a small bundle of second-hand clothing that had been generously donated by other families. We were never allowed into this other room to choose anything, we just had to take what we given. Once mum had loaded up the pram we set off home. Left along the High Street a hundred yards or so, left at the Post Office into Chandos Street another hundred yards or so then left at the Drill Hall into Wellington Street (none of this exists anymore, it's just a mass of concrete) this route kept us of the High Street probably because it was quicker or possibly to save us from any embarrassment. Along Wellington Street (which ran parallel to the High Street and right into Mackenzie Street towards the railway station; we were away, until I spotted some Grammar School Boys all toffed-up in their uniforms and carrying briefcases. I could tell they were up to something, it was awful. What would they do? As we drew closer they began to smirk and as we passed they began singing the tune to 'Steptoe & Son' you know, the 'Rag &Bone' men on the telly. That was so cruel! I don't think poor little Jim noticed and my mum certainly paid no attention. She just kept pushing that pram with us beside her.

Despite all I've just mentioned, it was in fact a good system, designed as a safety net for poor unfortunate families. Where would we have been without it? Christmas! I mustn't forget Christmas. The build up to Christmas in Juniors school was absolutely fantastic. There were the Nativity plays, the ice-slides in the playground and the parties in the classrooms. Mr Devine was a very kind man. He was a senior welfare officer who'd call at the house and ask us what we wanted for Christmas and do his best not to disappoint us, but I'm afraid that there wasn't much on offer, and we'd probably end up with a selection of second-hand books. All in all though, it was the kindness and the generosity that has impacted on me mostly. Ordinary people who had probably struggled themselves, reached out to the less fortunate.

Amongst the Trades vehicles that used to come down our street therel there was one in particular; a bright yellow van with name 'Cleener Kleener'; something like that. It was an unusual spelling and the man who drove it was only quite young himself. Well, he use to collect all the items for 'dry-cleaning' and one day, probably a Saturday he asked us if we were going on holiday, to which we replied 'no'. He went up to the house and spoke to my mum and the next thing we knew was that it had been arranged for us to stay at his house in West Drayton with his family. I was very young but I can remember the house distinctly. It had a hallway, a front room with a dining table where had our meals, a very comfortable back room with a television, French windows and a wooden conservatory containing plants and flowers and a small neat kitchen. In the back garden was a garage with an access drive running behind the houses. I don't remember their names but he would go off to work in his car and we would stay with his young wife and two children. I can't even remember how long we stayed for, it might have been a week or a long weekend but I do remember watching Bill and Ben the flowerpot men and listening to the music while the test-card was being broadcast. There was a small back lawn where we'd play in one of those toy pedal cars; that was great fun and the shops were quite close and we all went shopping for groceries at least once. Although I was very young, probably four or five, it was a happy and memorable occasion

On a regular basis my younger brother, myself and my sister were picked up by welfare officers, and taken out on day trips by coach with other children, or holidays to the seaside for a week or two. Swanage was a place we went to when we were very young. We stayed in huts, slept in bunk beds and walked everywhere. It was buckets and spades, Punch and Judy and ice creams. And if we didn't go to the seaside it would be cliff top walks. I remember the weather being very nice, and returning back to camp tired and hungry just in time for tea. I don't remember too much because I was quite young, but there were certain smells of flowers and, a certain brand of sun tan lotion that if I smell now take me straight back there in an instant and invoke pleasant memories.

Here is a copy of the letter card (3d) sent to my Mum by my sister:

Mrs. Wight
20, Belfast Avenue,
Slough,
Bucks.

Dear mummy I like it here very much. But I will be glad to come home on Friday and see you all. Kenny and Jimmy are getting on all right. Dear Mummy we play on the sand we watch punch and Judy we went on two boats at the sea-side.
That bit was from Kenny starting from Dear Mummy
I am spending my money wisely.
We went on two boats it was smashing we go to the beach every day and go into the sea.
Then we go and watch punch and Judy and if we like they buy us sweets and ice cream and I look after Kenny and Jim.
I will be very glad to see you because I miss you very much.
Lots of love From Rita Ken and Jim
xxxxxxxxxxxxxxxxxxxxxxxxxx

Rita is two years older than me but was probably less than 10 years old at this time.

When you think about those early days of national assistance and welfare officers it's hard to see how it has improved for the better, with its social workers and benefits system. It appears that for many, it has become a lifestyle choice. That's very sad.

Growing up

It must have been the first day of junior school, probably after the summer holidays, that my mum took me to school and for some reason all my sisters had left and I was taken in later because there was nobody in the streets. I suspect it would have been about 9.30am. I think for that reason I was terrified of going into school and the first attempt failed, but a detour to 'Bowyer's' the local shop for a bag of sweets did the trick and I settled in quite well with the help of Mrs Clark my first teacher at Godolphin Juniors.

In her class we did lots of spelling exercises which we copied out from the blackboard. We were issued with wooden one foot rulers, wooden ink pens and a nib, along with ink-pots that were placed into inkwells in our desks, some of the kids had fountain pens, but the Bic Biro which had just become available was not to be used and, finally, a small square of blotting paper to blot our work with. Tests were held regularly as well as daily recitals of the 'times tables' then at the end of the week stars of different colours were awarded and stuck onto a wall chart; gold being the highest. Every aspect of school life was carried out in an orderly and enjoyable fashion, from playground whistles, morning assemblies in the hall, to the dinnertime bell at 12 midday, and, of course, corporal punishment which, surprisingly, was very rare.

So looking back, I believe that the system was very good; I never felt frightened or threatened in any way, quite the opposite. We were looked after and disciplined, which made us respect authority, but having said this, there were one or two children with possibly, behavioural problems that were whisked out of mainstream education immediately. Unruly children in school were not tolerated and would not have been allowed to disrupt the main group. It's a bit different now isn't it, where the 'unruly' minority appear to rule supreme? It is often said that school days are the best days of your life, and that was certainly true for me during my junior years at Godolphin.

One of the highlights of the day was in the playground before dinner. The whistle would be blown once and we had to 'freeze' and stay perfectly still until the next whistle, when the children were then urged to use the toilet. There were no 'unhealthy' indoor toilets; the ones we used in the playground didn't even have a roof, although there were covers over the cubicles. We were then formed into a straight line in pairs, ready to walk down, escorted, to the dinner hall a ten minute walk away at Baylis Court senior girls school. Each day, our meal was preceded by saying grace, 'For what we are about to receive may the

Lord make us truly thankful, Amen'.

We were provided with a proper hot meal followed by pudding which would typically be something like jam roly-poly with custard. Mmm, delicious! No junk food then. During the course of the day I discovered that my best friend Harold, who lived next door but one, was in the next classroom, and that two of my sisters were further along. My new school was going to be fun, my confidence was rising comfortably and I was feeling good. Godolphin was a great school, all the teachers were different – some were young and trendy and others were older but more steady. The headmaster Mr Spinks was a disciplinarian and quite strict; if we ever passed him in the corridor we made sure that we marched on the left in single file and went quietly. It didn't seem to bother any of the children though, but we did think that he must have been important because he was the only teacher with a car which he parked right outside the school gate. I can remember it well; a small black round-shaped 'Austin of England' probably an A30, because it was the only one in the street.

The Deputy-Head Mr Lane (Pop Lane) an ex RAF type, tall with slicked back hair and a handlebar moustache, on the other hand, was a much more down to earth sort who always seemed to be in control in a more visible approachable way. He wore a tweed jacket with leather patches on the elbows, and I could never decide whether they were to protect the elbows from wearing thin, or a design feature. He taught in his own class at the other end of the corridor to final year pupils and kept the cane in his cupboard; he was responsible for keeping discipline. Though, in the four years that I spent there I only saw him give the 'whack' on two or three occasions and, regrettably, on one of those it was to me.

It was my own fault, because I had a one off opportunity to go for a family car ride with my uncle, but decided to go out with my friend Harold instead. It was during the Easter break whilst out playing that I let my friend talk me into climbing over the school fence into the playground and up onto the flat part of the roof of the school. It was quite low really, just the height of the porch, but I was scared and didn't enjoy the adventure at all because the school was empty and quiet and I knew that we shouldn't be there.

Anyway, unbeknown to us, we were spotted by the caretaker and picked out of our lines on the morning of the first day back. I can't describe the feeling of horror that I felt! We were escorted from there into the school and made to wait outside Mr Lane's classroom until the rest of the school had filed in and settled into their classrooms. How humiliating? When the hustle and bustle died down you could almost hear a pin drop. The waiting was nerve-racking, it was only a few minutes but it felt like an age. I was feeling full of regret at how I could have been so stupid. Mr Lane was the last person to walk in; the wait was over so I began to feel better. The punishment was a good telling off followed by two strokes of the cane on each hand, right on the fingertips, but it was nothing compared to waiting. All the same, it taught me a lesson, had no ill effects on me and thankfully, I never had to appear in front of him again. All in all the school was good to me and full of wonderful childhood memories.

The best advice to give to children is: when school is finished keep well away! although it's not always a guarantee for keeping out of trouble. You see, unlike today's children who spend most of their time in their bedrooms playing computer games, we only went upstairs to sleep. The rest of the time we were out usually getting up to mischief. Knock-down ginger was a good wheeze, but don't get caught because it usually ends up with a thick ear or worse. Me and Monty thought we'd try it for a laugh. We picked a house near the end of the street so as to make good our escape, we then rapped on the door and ran into the next street to hide in someone's garden, but the man was too quick for us. He dragged us from behind the hedge by the scruff of our neck, shouting and screaming at us in half Italian half English, at the top of his voice and then bashed our heads together.

The Police were called, and arrived in a Black Maria (a police van used to transport prisoners) to escort us home. It was shameful and embarrasing. We were both bawling, and had lumps the size of golf balls on our foreheads. We didn't do any more of that for fun, we sort of lost interest.

There were plenty more interesting adventures to be had. I lived at the hub of a thriving community where everything was in walking distance, including all the schools; no school runs to worry about; a ten or fifteen minute walk in any direction would get you to either, a parade of shops on the Farnham Road, equal to any high street if you didn't feel like getting the bus into town, which had a 'Picture House' as we used to call it; great for Saturday morning pictures which started about 10am with a 'serial' that wasn't to be missed; same time; at this cinema; next week! Following that was a full length film featuring Laurel and Hardy, Norman Wisdom, or George Formby. At the end of the film they played one or two cartoons. Smashing!

There were two Barbers, two Doctors surgeries, two chemists, two Fish and Chip shops, and Woolworths, where we could buy a bag of broken biscuits for a penny; it was all there, right on the doorstep.

There was no need for car, or multi-story car parks, the shopping was just carried in a rack under the baby's pram; of course, the weekly-shop was only a fraction of what it is by today's standards, and most stuff was delivered to the door in any case. Or there was the Orchard Youth Club, which cost a shilling (5p) to get in, that we used to go to every week day night, until the age of 21. There were two more Cinemas in town and one in Cippenham just outside of town in the opposite direction called the Essoldo that was built in the Art Deco style. Out of a total of four cinemas within easy reach, only the Adelphi remains as a Bingo Hall. I suppose we should count our blessings really, because that one could have met the same fate as the others. Okay, we have the modern multiplex version of the 'Picture Palace' but they're not the same somehow. There was the huge Slough Trading Estate; great for kids, because all the sweet factories were there, with no security in those days. We'd just walk up to the open doors and ask for sweets. As easy as that!

We were always up the Farnham Road for something or other, and one day when my sister was taking me for a haircut I heard a loud, continuous sound, like a ship's fog horn, and a few minutes later, hundreds of people on bicycles. I found out that the sound was the 'Factories' Hooter' that sounded three times a day; at 8am, 1pm and 5pm. You often hear nowadays that it's not safe to let children out on their own, that, 'when we were young we'd be out all day and only come back before dark'. Well that's exactly how it was; it was safer on the streets, the law was tougher and there were Policemen everywhere. The public were encouraged to get involved and were backed up by the law. Hooliganism and yobbish behaviour were not tolerated and capital punishment still existed for murder, Borstal for really bad boys, and National Service for 18 year olds which made for a much more ordered society with respect for authority and your elders.

In Belfast Avenue where I lived was the Boys Club, with its own cycle track, which carried on all sorts of activities from Football and Judo, to Youth Club and jumble sales. In the next street was the Social Centre with its own indoor Pool where I learnt to swim with the school. Mr Hurn, a huge Welshman our RE teacher and Games master, who wouldn't look out of place on the Welsh rugby team, (who incidentally brought rugby to William Penn and established a formidable school team) would, once a week, lead dozens of kids from school along the 'Cinder Track' to the pool, a good 20 minute walk, with one or two other teachers as assistants, to be instructed, tested and issued with certificates. It was optional, but we thought, a good dodge from lessons. Were the Teachers going soft?

Another great adventure was to try and reach the River Thames at Windsor; that was an all day jaunt and my favourite pursuit. The quickest and most direct route was across the field.

We were surrounded by parks which were patrolled by Park Keepers on bicycles. Godolphin Park (the field) was the nearest, which led straight into Baylis Park, connected by streams that we used to jump across or swing across on ropes (we got that idea from the 'Tarzan' films). Baylis was a beautiful mature wooded park with a lake where we'd fish for tadpoles, sticklebacks and newts with our homemade nets made from a stick and one of our sister's old stockings.

The parks were our playground and we felt perfectly safe in them because there were always people walking their dogs, couples strolling, families picnicking or just other kids like us playing. One happy occasion that I'll never forget was when Mr Deverill (Reg) my friend Allan's Dad took us to the lake. It was so much better to go with an adult and felt like more of an occasion. When we got back, we put our fish into buckets, our newts into shallow bowls with rocks in, so they could climb out of the water, and flushed the dead ones down the toilet.

Allan's Gran gave us a cake and a drink and allowed us to watch 'Popeye' on the set in the front room. What a treat! And Popeye was my favourite program of all time.

The outside swimming pool was here too, where on the hot summer days, we'd spend quite a lot of time. In the autumn, Baylis Park was the best place for collecting conkers, all under the watchful eye of the park-keeper 'the Parky', George, who rode a policeman's bicycle. He was a big portly man in a cap and tunic; most people in authoritative positions wore a uniform including Bus Drivers and Conductors, Cinema Commissionaires and Ambulance Drivers.

Leaving Baylis and continuing on under the railway bridge took you into Salt Hill Park recreation area (the 'rec'), the land, funds and buildings of which were donated to Slough by James Elliman in 1907, who founded and manufactured "Elliman's Embrocation", a rub for sprained muscles. It was a beautiful park with a large paddling pool, changing rooms and toilets, a café, tennis courts, and football pitches. It was a good place for families and picnics.

If you reached the far side of the park, you only needed to cross the A4 to get to the Town Hall on the other side to pay the rent if you had missed the rent man. My mum said that paying the rent each fortnight and never getting into arrears was more important than buying food or coal. How could that be? We needed to eat and keep warm! I swore on that day that I would buy my own house when I was older and never pay rent to anyone. Anyway, if you turned left at the park gates it was only a short walk from there into town, and that was usually the way we would go.

Behind the Town hall was Montem Park. The first time I saw it, I was amazed at how grand it looked. The mown lawns which cascaded down to a boating lake were surrounded at the entrance by high cast iron gates and railings; if you continued past the lake it would lead to a tree lined footpath that veered left beside the stream that exited in the far corner. Emerging from the park amongst the trees, without any warning, was the picturesque Victorian Village of Chalvey with shops, pubs, a church and a horse and cart. It was 'picture postcard' beautiful; a glimpse into the past, that was the original settlement and more sedate version of Slough High Street.

After a brief spell there looking at all the equipment in the Army Surplus Store, it was on to the footpath which ran beside the Windsor Branch Line; a great place for gooseberry picking. At some point after that, the line was raised up onto the '100 Arches' that cut through allotments, Eton College playing fields and finally over the Thames into Winsor Central Station. The footpath finished on the 'Brocas' beside the river on the Eton side, we'd achieved our mission, now it was time to explore! After the river, Windsor Castle was the big attraction. There were punts taking people across for a penny, but we didn't have any money, so we walked a few hundred yards towards Eton High Street and over the bridge, but before we crossed over we explored the High Street; if anyone is planning a trip to Windsor, be sure to include this in your itinerary. It's a marvellous place straight out of a Dickens novel; with its old restaurants and shops, bespoke Tailors, College Boys walking about in their morning suits, and of course, Eton College. The scene is set!

Over the bridge into Windsor, and up castle hill is a sight to behold. Back then, tourists were free to walk in and out all day long, but nowadays, security is tight and there's an entrance charge. Once inside the Castle walls you're pretty much free to wander where you please, except where the Queen lives, and is there most weekends. You will see Her and Prince Philip, and other members of the Royal Family close up, sometimes quite unexpectedly, as I have done on numerous occasions. I and my friends were fortunate enough to climb the tight spiral staircase of the Round Tower to reach the top of the highest point in the Castle where the flags are flown. It's exhausting, but well worth it. Fantastic!

Can you imagine it? You can't do it now though, because it's been closed to the public for health and safety reasons. I think the Guard is changed every day now, and that is something that must not be missed; they look resplendent in their red tunics, accompanied by the marching band, through Windsor and up into the Castle.

Whilst in the Castle recently with my young son, a troop of Guardsmen were marching towards us at a pace; my son gripped my hand and asked: 'Dad, what do they do if we're in the way' well we soon found out; the Sergeant marching by their side bellowed at the top of his voice: 'MAKE WAY FOR THE QUEENS GUARD!' to the sheer enjoyment of the crowd. I visit Windsor frequently; it's a place I never tire of.

As my sisters got older and started work (at 15 years old) we were able to have one or two nice things in the house. Each week they would bring home a lamp shade, some towels or ornaments, small things like that. My mum was also able to pay a few shillings into a club each week, then when we had enough to buy a larger item, they would issue us with vouchers to spend in certain selected shops; that's how we got our first piece of oilcloth to cover the boards in the front room, and a woven plastic mat for the stone floor in the scullery. The kitchen or, scullery, as my mum called it had a stone floor, a cast iron gas stove, a Belfast sink, a wooden draining board and an electric light; that was it! No electric power points and no electrical appliances.

There was a gas 'Copper Boiler' under the draining board for washing the clothes that were then hung over a line in the kitchen to dry; my mum would usually speed up the drying process by turning on all the gases on the stove. The lavatory was outside the back door with no light or window just a six inch gap at the top and bottom of the door for light and ventilation; we kids managed alright but my mum used to take in an oil lamp or candle after dark. At bedtime the doors were bolted and weren't opened again until the morning, so in case anyone needed to go in the night a bucket was placed on the landing and emptied in the morning.

When I got older I talked to my friends and neighbours of this odd routine, and was surprised to hear that they did the very same thing. The pantry (larder) had a cold shelf which comprised a four inch thick concrete shelf, and a six inch square opening at the top for ventilation, with a grill on the outside, and wire mesh on the inside to stop flies and insects from getting in; and you'd be surprised how cool that used to be. If it was very hot we'd put the bottles of milk into a bowl of cold water placed on the stone floor of the larder; that would keep them fresh for longer.

In 1960 my older sister was courting her future husband, Mick Joel who lived in Dedworth near Windsor, we had the address so we decided to go and see where he lived; all we needed were directions. It was a nice sunny day during the school holidays, so me and my brother went there together; it was the first time I ever walked to Windsor, I was 9 years old and he was 7. I knew how to get there because we had been there several times before with our mum on family trips; my mum would push the pram with me and my brother in it, when we were little, and the girls would walk either side, then she would take the route by road.

It was easy really; you just had to get into Slough and then take the Windsor Road. When we reached the Castle we rested on the benches outside, we had no food, drink or money so we just sat for a while.

Then I noticed a brown paper bag on the bench next to us and inside was a brand new pair of men's brogues. In those days a policeman was the first port of call for any inquiry; from asking directions, the time of day, or seeing people across the road, to reporting bad or suspicious behaviour. Nearby at the crossroads in front of the Castle was a policeman on point's duty, so off together with the bag we went. He was a typical 'Dixon of Dock Green' (TV program) character; middle-aged, big and imposing, but professional and attentive to our needs; he actually halted all the traffic to talk to us. Then told us to hand the shoes in to the Police station as he had to stay with the traffic, but because we didn't know where it was, and I'll never forget what he did next! He put his hand up to stop the 441, a double-decker bus, spoke to the driver, then put us on the back telling the conductor to put us off at the Police station which, incidentally, wasn't that far away, about half a mile, but we felt really important.

My mum would say 'mark my words, if you do wrong you will always get paid back, and likewise, if you are kind and helpful you will be rewarded, because a good heart never wants for long'. These wise words were sound tenets that I live my life by and pass on to my son today, and firmly believe they have guided me and put me in good stead. Over the years I have met people who believe that they deserve what others have worked hard for, but aren't prepared to make the same effort themselves, thinking that there is easy money to be had by stealing or ripping people off. It may be true, and that way probably does provide 'easy money' in the short term, but ultimately, crime doesn't pay! My teenage son always needs money for something, which I provide, but he has to earn it first. I tell him that all that is necessary for a good life is to be honest and work hard, frequently reminding him that it is a well known maxim he would do well to observe.

From there we asked for directions to Vale road, Dedworth and carried on. When we arrived, my, now, brother-in-law's parents were amazed that two small boys had made that long journey alone, and because we didn't have phones we were kept there until my sister turned up. I bet she was pleased? In the meantime we were led into the kitchen to wash our hands in the sink. Surprisingly, although their sitting room was quite comfortable, their kitchen was utilitarian. Not dissimilar to ours at home; dark green walls, with a dim electric light, hanging from the ceiling over a well worn, dark concrete floor. Under the Crittall 'Cottage Pane' window was a Belfast sink (a standard fitment in council houses of the time) with a cold tap and pipe-work clipped to the surface above it. Mick's mother informed us that the council were coming to modernise the kitchen next week; we're getting a hot tap! Afterwards, we ate banana sandwiches and drank tea, then at 5 o'clock the telly went on and we watched 'Bonanza' for the first time. Not bad for a day out, eh?

*

When I was quite young, up until about the age of 6 or 7, although we didn't have a telly, we did have a wireless that I remember listening to on a Sunday morning. It was a programme full of messages and requests for and from British forces posted abroad at BFPO, which played tunes by Frank Sinatra, and Doris Day etc. Not very interesting listening for children's ears; in fact I found it extremely boring. Then new songs began coming though by artists such as Jim Reeves (my mum's favourite) Lonnie Donnegan, and Tommy Steele, which were much more upbeat and interesting; definitely a change for the better, but it was only to be for a short period, because this was the late 1950's, just before the Rock and Roll explosion.

The first time Mick Joel came to our house my brother Jim and I hid under the table; we were very exited but didn't want to be seen. Were we scared or shy? I can't remember! I do remember that my sisters were just teenagers, and had recently bought a record player and some records. It was the age of the 'Teddy boy' and there was a new sound called 'Rock and Roll'. The kind of songs they liked to play were by Elvis and Buddy Holly. What a sound! Jailhouse Rock, Oh Boy and many others.

As the music played, we waited at the window for Mick and his friend 'Little Mick' to arrive that Saturday afternoon. We suddenly saw them walking down the street towards our front gate. They looked like film stars with their Brylcreamed quiffs and DA hairstyles; they wore dark drape jackets and bootlace ties, drainpipe trousers and winkle picker shoes. When they knocked on the door, that's when we darted for cover.

As time went on he became one of the family, he was an instant success with my mum, like an older brother to us, and my Gran and Granddad loved him. He worked very hard; his job was in an Iron Foundry, die-casting, but every time he came to our house he was always immaculately turned out in a suit and tie, and wore gold cufflinks. We looked up to him, and as the only adult male in the family he sort of became the man of the house.

They married two years later, and although he is now officially retired he can still graft and he still has his Teddy boy haircut.

When I saw him just recently, he told me something that I would like to share with you. I wanted to know what the procedure was to become a council tenant. 'Well first' he said 'we had to prove that we were married before going onto the housing list, where there were many families ahead of us'. The only option was to find lodgings until something became available. My sister would be responsible for locating suitable accommodation, and found a very nice comfortable 'bedsit' in Sussex Place. It comprised two rooms on the top floor of a large Victorian villa, with a landing leading to a kitchen, toilet and bathroom. Very desirable!

On their first Christmas, they decided to stay at Mick's Mum's in Vale Road. The 'newlyweds' had a marvellous day and were very happy to be with their family. By the end of the day they said 'goodnight all' and got up to go to bed. 'Where are we sleeping mother?' 'You're in with Dad and June's in with me'. Well, he said it was a bit of a shock; after all, we were married. Next day they made their excuses and set off back to Slough, on foot; there were no buses on Boxing Day back then.

*

Boys will be boys! That was a term frequently heard because, inevitably, left to our own devices, we would get into trouble. Like the time me and my friend and classmate Colin Skuta (Polish) walked into some new shops that were being built on the Farnham Road; there were no fences or security and no workmen, just a building site left totally open to the street that was too much of a temptation for small boys to explore, but in those days I expect that we were to be trusted and should have known better.

Anyway, there was building material everywhere and we found an open box of shiny new nails from which we began to fill our pockets, thinking that they would be useful in building a camp or a trolley; big mistake!

Then off we went to get some wood from the Farnham Road, you pretty much get anywhere and anything because it bordered the Trading Estate, and you only had to ask.

Danvis's wood mill was a few hundred yards along on the opposite side of the road, next to the GWR line with its own sidings, a dedicated track with its own station to bring people in to work, which weaved around the estate; its small steam (tank) engine would collect goods wagons from the factories and return the empties.

Again no fences; we were free to wander unhindered along the tracks and into the mill as we'd done many times before. The workmen there were friendly and would fill our cart with off-cuts of wood; sometimes 3 or 4 feet long.

On route to Danvis's was the Chix factory, that made chewing gum and sweet cigarettes, where two of my sisters worked, so we'd stop there first and ask the man for some sweets. Before we had the chance to do that, and to every young boy's horror, we bumped into a Policeman on a bicycle, and there we stood stunned like rabbits caught in headlights.

He wasn't concerned that we were around the factories, but he did want to know what was in our bulging pockets; we told him about the building site down the road, he asked us to show him where we found the nails and told us to put them back. That would have been a relief if that had been the end of it, but no, he then walked us home to tell our parents.

Let me just explain what it was like back then for those too young to remember. Although we lived in a large industrial town, it wasn't overcrowded as it is now, teeming with people of every nationality. There were Polish and Italian families that had settled here after the war, which at that time was then only 15 odd years ago, they lived in their own privately bought houses that were nicely painted and immaculately kept, with fine gardens. They worked hard and fully supported themselves and their families; there were no lavish benefits and handouts for them or for anyone else for that matter.

We went to school with their children who spoke perfect English and you would only know they were foreign when you heard their names. We all knew who was who, and who lived where. What a great immigration policy! Totally integrated, self-dependent and accounted for. Policemen were highly respected pillars of the community and the last thing that you wanted was to cross their path; if you were unfortunate and did get nabbed it was humiliating for you and your family.

*

Most kids went scrumping for apples, pears or cherries. I don't think it was a crime, but you didn't want to get caught on someone's property stealing from their garden, because you were likely to get a good hiding.

One day when I went out with my friend Monty, getting up to the usual mischief, he thought he would take a chance on the orchard next to the college. I didn't know if it was private property or not, but I did know that Fatty Arbuckle, the Rag and Bone man kept his horse there, and wouldn't take kindly to trespassers. I warned him! But, nevertheless, over the gate he went and made for the nearest apple tree. I was having none of it; I stayed outside on the other side of the gate. Fatty Arbuckle was 6ft tall and 6ft round and had a reputation. Anyway, halfway up the tree there was Monty, tongue hanging out, filling his pockets when all of a sudden Fatty appeared; 'Oi!!' he bellowed. Fatty was too close for Monty to make a run for it, so he scrambled higher up into the tree; Fatty had a long reach though, and grabbed Monty by the ankle, and with a yank pulled him crashing to the ground, while with his other hand, unfastening the thick leather belt from around his waist, vigorously administered to Monty a sound thrashing.

It was great to watch, and didn't bother Monty at all, he was as tough as old boots and just glad to get away. We laughed and talked about it all the way home, and for months afterwards.

*

When I was about 10 years old my oldest sister's boyfriend got us our first telly. It was a second hand console model with a tiny screen that would only show one channel, and could only be viewed very poorly if the indoor aerial had been placed in the right position.

Every 10 minutes or so the vertical hold would go, leaving us with an unwatchable screen, then one of us, usually me, would have to go to the back of the set to adjust the picture. In this way we were able to watch an early episode of Coronation Street.

Who can remember the scene in the 'Snug' at the Rovers Return, with Minnie Caldwell and Martha Longhurst, sitting around a small table with their half pints of Milk Stout, being domineered by Ena Sharples?

We had only ever watched a screen at the pictures so that's how we sat, in rows in front of this telly with the lights out and the curtains closed. After about an hour, we got bored of sitting there, turned it off, and then got back to normal. That poor old telly struggled on for about a month then gave up.

We had one or two old sets given to us every now and then, but didn't seriously bother again until we rented one in the late 1960's.

I could usually watch telly in my friend's house in any case, so I didn't really miss out. On those occasions when we did have access to a television the favourites of the day were: Emergency ward 10, Z cars, Harry Worth, and so on.

There were no feature films shown, except for old Black and White war films on Sunday afternoons; broadcasting ended with the national anthem at 10pm and a voice that said: 'Please turn off your set!', the frame would collapse into a bright white dot in the middle of the screen that we would watch until it disappeared.

Anyway I preferred to go to the pictures every week, it was more exciting because you got to go out, see all your friends and watch a great film on a big screen, more often than not, in colour. It wasn't that expensive either. Saturday morning pictures was 6d and at other times 1/-. Among the dozens of memorable films we watched were: 101 Dalmatians, The Lady and the Tramp, Summer Holiday, with Cliff Richard and many more.

When the film Zulu was first released I went to see it twice in the same week, and since then, many times over. It really is an amazing film based on facts. The following dialogue at the beginning of the film is narrated by Richard Burton, who reads:

The Secretary of State for War has today received the following dispatch from Lord Chelmsford, Commander-in-Chief of Her Majesty's forces in Natal colony, South Africa.

I regret to report a very disastrous engagement which took place on the morning of the 22nd of January between the armies of the Zulu king Cetshwayo and our own Number 3 Column, consisting of Five Companies of the 1st Battalion, 24th Regiment of Foot, and one company of the 2nd Battalion, a total of nearly 1,500 men, officers and other ranks."

"The Zulus, in overwhelming numbers, launched a highly disciplined attack on the slopes of the mountain of ISANDHLWANA, and in spite of gallant resistance...The column was completely annihilated

As well as watching it on telly, I have since bought it on DVD and almost know the script off by heart.

Dutchy: 'Alright! How far can you rednecks march in a day?'

Jones 716: 'oh! 15, 20 miles is it'

Dutchy: 'well a Zulu regiment can run! RUN! 50 miles, and fight a battle at the end of it'.

Jones 593: 'Well there's daft it is then, I don't see no sense in running to fight a battle'.

The films were advertised on 3ft square bill boards located around the town and outside the cinemas, and there was one of those boards at the end of our street; easy! The coloured posters were ever so exiting. I can see them now; 'the Day of the Triffids' that was scary, or 'Doctor Who and the Daleks', with William Hartnell as the Doctor.

At the cinema, forthcoming films were advertised with the use of 'trailers' and the plot was never given away as so happens today, all too frequently. The film, the 'Planet of the Apes' for example, told the story of astronauts landing on an alien planet where the Apes ruled the Humans. It is only at the end, when Taylor escapes on horseback along a sandy beach that he sees the Statue of Liberty collapsed and protruding though the sand, that he (and the audience) realise that they had really landed back on earth in the future. It had the most staggering effect on me and my friends as we left after the film.

*

There were only two TV channels on the 405-lines VHF system; the picture being scanned across the screen with interlacing lines, with just as much gap in between each of the lines, was at the time of its introduction referred to as the "high definition" 405-line system, that was just about watchable with an indoor aerial, and only in black and white. In 1964 the BBC launched its BBC2 service on UHF using a 625-line system adding more picture lines, and so reducing the amount of gaps, giving a much better picture with improved definition, which was also compatible with colour transmission that was later broadcast at the end of the 1960's.

It was the early days of colour TV in Britain, the sets were much more expensive, needed a different type of aerial (UHF), and required a more expensive TV licence. So the take-up was slow in the beginning, but by the mid seventies colour sets were improved upon and became more affordable.

Black and white tellies were seen as old fashioned and more and more people began to replace them with a new colour set, the Japanese models being way ahead of their Western rivals in technology, reliability and performance. Many people who purchased colour televisions didn't change their black and white licences to colour licences because of the extra cost, and when the detector van came round they merely turned the colour off to avoid detection!

The last 405-line transmissions were seen on the 3rd January, 1985 and with that the separate licensing was abolished and only one TV licence was available.

In our street you could tell who had a TV set by looking up at their chimney stack to see if there was an aerial up on it. I suppose in the entire street there were less than ten houses with rooftop aerials, although this wasn't an accurate indicator as to who had a telly, because many people went for an indoor aerial as a cheaper option.

My friend Harold's parents (Mr and Mrs Bampton) were one of the first families to get the new TV with the extra channel (BBC 2) in 1964; the giveaway was the different shape of aerial, required to receive the UHF frequency necessary for the 625-lines television receiver. Very posh! Second to the extra channel, the most obvious improvement was in the advanced picture quality.

Unlike our household, the Bampton's house was a model family dwelling; a two parent family, both working, with three children, nice furniture, rugs on the floor and carpet on the stairs; kept spotless by a cylinder 'Hoover', the very popular and modern 'must have' labour saving appliance of the day. They even had a single electric socket fitted in the kitchen, which was a marvel, because those houses only came with electric lighting, and one 5amp, two pin socket, in the front room as standard. If you had an electric iron it had to be plugged into the light socket; the problem here though, was that it did not provide an earth, and unlike a screw bulb socket, could not be polarised (connect the wrong way round). Later, revised electrical regulations rendered this practice obsolete due to safety reasons.

Theirs was an end of terrace house with space at the side for a garage, although they never owned a car in the early days, and a huge 100ft garden at the back with a duck pond and a vegetable plot. They were the best people in the whole world to me, a good friend and neighbour to my mum, and where I spent most of my time, and had many memorable occasions.

Like the time they took me with them on a coach trip to Littlehampton for the day, where me and Harold tried to get to France in a pedal boat. We could see a faint outline and it didn't look that far away; we thought we could get there in a couple of hours. After about five minutes we got tired, and when we looked behind and saw how far out we were, got scared and turned back.

I swear that Harold didn't have a nerve in his body, he was a real dare devil. He climbed an old oak tree in the park, that no one I knew could ever manage, but on the way up he disturbed a wasp's nest and was afraid to come back down. He told one of us to run back across the field to fetch his Dad; we showed Mr Bampton (Ralph) where Harold was trapped by the swarming wasps and without further ado, he scrambled up the tree and brought Harold down on his shoulder. What a great man! We asked him why he didn't get stung, and he replied that the wasps were his friends; that in the past when he had a bad back, he had been stung by a wasp, and was healed.

To us though, he was a real hero, a role model, someone to look up to. I mean that literally, he was a roofer by trade, 6 foot tall, as brown as a berry and as fit as a fiddle with a kind and pleasing disposition. Ralph enlisted with the Royal Berkshire Regiment in 1938, Birmingham.

Army no. 5336906. His training was with the Royal Fusiliers in 1939 and with the Essex Regiment in 1942 and was sent out to the Middle East in 1944 where he transferred to the Highland Light Infantry. He was awarded the War Medal, and The Italy Star which was awarded to only those who fought in Italy between 1943/45. Ralph was demobbed on the 8th November 1946.

On past the old oak tree towards the GWR main line was the site known as 'Limmer and Trinidad' which occupied quite a few acres of disused land that was mainly concreted over; this is where we used to ride old motor bikes off-road before we were old enough to have a licence.

Allan Deverill, who lived at the opposite end of the terrace, and still does, was always mechanically minded even from a young age, and was always tinkering with cars or repairing motor bikes.

At the age of about 14, he had a great knack of acquiring old non-runners from the backs of people's gardens that had probably lain there for years. He never paid more than a fiver for them and we'd often see him pushing an old motorbike down the street, back to his house. Once he got them running, it was off to 'Limmer and Trinidad' where we would just run them into the ground and then acquire another one.

There seemed to be an unlimited supply of these old bikes. I believe it was because it was the mid-sixties and car ownership was on the increase. Those old bikes are now highly sought after by collectors and enthusiasts, who regularly pay thousands of pounds for them.

At the far edge of the site close to the sidings were some industrial buildings. One of these was huge, with no doors at either end, a railway track ran through it, and approximately 50 feet above was an overhead crane. There was never anyone around, and I'm not sure if that site was still in use; there were no gates or effective fencing surrounding the place so it just became another place to explore, a playground. I suppose, not dissimilar to the bomb-sites in London at that time.

No adults would ever think of wandering on to that site, it just looked derelict and would have been of no interest to them. The police, though, were always checking on us; their main concern was that we didn't attempt to ride the bikes on the public highway or dash from there across the field to home. So providing we did as we were told there wasn't much they could do.

It's a good job they didn't catch Harold climbing up the 50ft steel ladder into the overhead crane, or see me and Monty climb on to the footplate of a GWR mainline steam engine whilst it was resting on the turntable. I can remember it vividly; it was 5pm on a cold winter's night, and in the darkness we could see the glow from the firebox, and could hear the hissing of the steam. It was too much; we had to go and investigate. We walked down some steps from the main road into complete darkness, save the glow coming from this huge magnificent steam engine; we imagined that we would like to have pulled some levers and ride down the track a bit, but that would have been impossible; we were too scared, thank God!

I often talk to my friend, who is a railways enthusiast, about that time, and he says that the engine was probably left unattended while the workmen were on their break, before being turned around to go back to London for repairs or other duties.

*

A superb annual event was the Slough Holiday Carnival held at Agars Plough – part of Eton playing fields - for two weeks every August. We'd often go down there during the day in the school holidays, and at certain times we didn't have to pay, but during the evenings there were huge crowds queuing to get in. The central display area designated for the circus, which included a High Wire trapeze act, and clowns and such like, was surrounded by marquees and tents which were provided for local societies and charities. There were other events like wrestling, and side shows and a fairground with an old fashioned Helter Skelter for 6d a go.

The last time that I went to Agars Plough was the morning after a massive gale the night before. The grounds looked like a whirlwind had swept through it. All the tents were either torn or down and the contents scattered about. It was an awful sight to see all their hard work destroyed, and to watch them trying to clear up the mess. They didn't appear to mind us milling about, but instead let us help ourselves to the various gateaux that hadn't been too badly damaged by the storm.

I must admit though, I felt quite guilty eating the cake, while they shuffled around the remains of their exhibits, looking so forlorn, so we quickly moved away. That could possibly have been the last time that the carnival took place as well, because we never went back there again.

When the Labour party's Hugh Gaitskell died unexpectedly in

January 1963 it left an opening for Harold Wilson in the party leadership. This was my 4th and last year at Juniors and, one morning in assembly, we were told that the Leader of the Labour party Harold Wilson would be coming to Slough to speak at a public meeting in Slough Technical School, which is literally at the end of our street next to the Boys club.

We were told the time and date and urged to attend; the weather was warm so I expect that it was around Easter time.

Anyway about 7 o'clock'ish a dozen or so of us made our way over to the school; we couldn't get inside because it was full, so the caretaker erected some trestles and boards for us to stand on near to the open windows on the outside. Was that wise for a group of 12 year olds? We weren't interested in politics we were just there for the fun of it.

Once in position one of the boys, Eric Wight (my cousin) proclaimed that he had an egg for Mr Wilson and without hesitation, lobbed it through the open window. It was a brilliant shot from approximately 20ft away, hitting the politician right between the eyes and running down his face. There was a gasp, and then all of us on the trestle froze, as the entire audience turned around to see where the egg had come from. Eric was quickly taken hold of and led away. With that, we cleared off.

Back at school in assembly the Headmaster addressed the pupils, informing them of the unfortunate event. It was decided not to punish the boy if, instead, he would write a letter of apology to Mr Wilson, which he eagerly agreed to do. Within a week the school had their reply from the kindly Mr Wilson, who took it all in good spirit and forgave the boy. Phew! It was in all the papers, making Eric a bit of a name for himself. The following year 1964 was election year. Labour won, and Harold Wilson served as Prime Minister.

Just before the school summer holidays a famous female star (they weren't called celebrities then) came to the boys club for some sort of event or other. All the local kids were there and so were the Press. She was making a fuss of all the kids but there was one child that caught her attention; that child was little Jimmy, my younger brother.

He was only about 7 with a mop of dark hair in a sort of a bob and big blue eyes. Very cute! She found him adorable, picked him up and gave him a cuddle saying that she wanted to adopt him. She probably thought that she would take him from rags and give him riches. With that, a posse of kids along with me and Jimmy charged down the street back home to tell my mum the story. We were quite surprised though, when she said: No! 'She can't have my little Jimmy, he's staying here'. Poor little Jim could have been famous!

Anyway a few days later the welfare officer called to the house to tell my mum that the famous person wanted to pay for a holiday for me and Jim. The place we were to go to was a boy's Holiday Camp in St Mary's Bay. On the day, we were collected from the house and taken to the station to go by train to Paddington, where we had to take a short walk to Ladbroke Grove to pick up our holiday coach. We didn't know any of the other kids because they were all from London. When we arrived at the Camp, we saw that it was several huts surrounding a huge paying field, quite close to the seafront.

Inside the hut that we were to stay in, were a dozen beds on either side each with a small locker, in other words, a dormitory with separate bedrooms for the staff. There was no entertainment, but there was a canteen serving three meals a day, and a film hut that we were taken to, to watch 'Treasure Island'; the 1950's version, with Robert Newton as 'Long John Silver'.

One of the many memorable occasions was a visit to Dover Castle, where we had a guided tour around the dungeons, and up onto the ramparts, from where we could see France, just twenty miles away across the Channel; was that foreign country that close we enquired?

A ride on the Romney, Hythe and Dymchurch miniature railway, during a trip to Dungeness, and up to the top of the lighthouse was great fun! We were well looked after, but also had plenty of free time to explore. When we were on the coach and it was time to leave, we all began to sing; it was a nice time.

It was during my fourth year at Godolphin that I sat my 11 plus exam. I loved this school and didn't want to leave, especially to go on to senior school, to become a first year pupil amongst all those grownups. I was three points short of a pass so instead of Slough Technical School, of the alternatives, I chose to go to William Penn Secondary Modern School for Boys, named after the seventeenth century Quaker and founder of Pennsylvania, because that was where all my friends were going.

The school and its housing estate were built at the same time in the 1930's. The school a 20 minute walk from my house, leaving through the back garden gate, out into and across Granville playing fields, along Granville Avenue and through Manor Park, to its most northern and highest point to Penn Road, where it was situated.

It commanded an unrestricted view across the whole of Slough in the Thames valley, and of Windsor Castle on the southern side of the River Thames; in fact they faced each other. Do you think this was maybe a deliberate ploy by the town planners, to somehow link the schools Christian heritage to the Monarchy?

Oh! And incidentally, Granville, (1761-1844) was the last Penn to own Stoke Park, was William Penn's grandson!

Moving up and not knowing what to expect made me feel quite apprehensive and nervous especially after hearing all the stories from the older boys, about how the Headmaster kept several canes of varying thickness on a rack on the wall of his study that were dispensed according to the level of punishment to be meted out, all of which, was then recorded in the punishment book. If any boys were caught fighting, the games master would haul them into the boxing ring, in the assembly hall, to fight it out fairly in front of the school. Instead of feeling scared, I felt that it was the correct and a proper way to handle 'fisticuffs' that started in the playground. It would also be properly monitored and controlled by a member of staff.

For lesser misdemeanours, like forgetting PE kit, homework etc, or being late, detention after school was the order of the day. I only had a couple of detentions throughout secondary school and one of those was presided over by the Deputy Headmaster Mr Halsey. We all thought it was going to be tough, but we were pleasantly surprised. Mr Halsey was a very kind man, who obviously loved his job, and compared to the other teachers he looked much older; I suspect, he would have been in his early 60's and quite resembled Mr. Chips in character and appearance.

Rather than a punishment, he made the detention fun by reciting a series of anecdotes. He then separated us into rows for a game of 'Chinese whispers' explaining to us how messages can become distorted if verbally relayed several times. It was an interesting exercise and great fun!

Finally he gave us a real live account of Chinese whispers, telling us of a runner in a battle who had to deliver the message 'send reinforcements, we're going to advance'. After the message had been relayed several times, it was finally received as: 'send three and fourpence, we're going to a dance'. For younger readers, three shillings and fourpence

3/4d in decimal money is equivalent to about 17 pence.

On my first day at William Penn as I stood in the playground with all my friends, I saw at the far end towards the back of the school, a huge mountain of coal. An oldish man in work clothes was shovelling the coal into a wheelbarrow. As he came towards us, I saw that he wore a bib and brace, work boots and gloves. He lifted a manhole cover close by, and then tipped the coal from the barrow into it; he then disappeared down some steps into the boiler room. That was Pop Price the caretaker.

While me and some friends waited outside talking to the older boys who lived down our street, and with my hands full of 'hundreds and thousands' one of them unknown to me, who lived on the estate, slapped the bottom of my hands sending the sweets flying. My immediate reaction was to punch him straight on the jaw and send him flying. Poor Jim (Jimmy Birkett), I regretted it immediately. No real harm done though, we were friends from then on and his brother Allan was my dinner monitor.

WILLIAM PENN COUNTY SECONDARY SCHOOL FOR BOYS,
Penn Road, SLOUGH

When the whistle was blown we lined up and were let in by a Prefect. As the door opened, I paused momentarily as I looked and saw inside my new school, it was with a feeling of excitement and anticipation.

The Last School Photo (1969)
Mr Hamlin Mr Mills Mr Johnson Mr Hurn
(centre wearing ties)

The first thing I noticed was the cast-iron radiator, the warmth, the clean smell, the polished floors and the fresh paintwork. It was a tough school, and had a reputation for being so, although, bullying was virtually non-existent because it was dealt with swiftly, usually by the older boys.

Built in 1936, as was most of that area, it was of a solid designed two storey facade in the shape of a square surrounding the assembly hall which had a small enclosed garden either side; very nice! All the internal corridor walls were windowed with small panes, typical of that era, which provided lots of natural light. The electric lighting, 'traditional tungsten filament' to use its technical description, (light bulbs to everyone else) gives off a soft warm yellow light, which is kind on the eye, atmospheric and functional; subdued in places but gave light where it was needed. Thankfully, we had no fluorescent lighting in our school then, so were spared the garish white, unnatural phosphorous emissions, from floor to ceiling, of those mercury discharge lamps.

What I see, everywhere I go these days, are masses of fluorescent lights, including the new compact fluorescent bulbs, that flood everything, including the ceiling, in a coarse harsh white light; is not very good on the eyes and has been known to trigger headaches, migraines and epileptic fits. Leaving that aside though, they are very efficient and are cheap to run. The disadvantages being, the initial high purchase cost, and the inconvenience of disposal. They can't just be placed in a normal dustbin; they have to be recycled, because of the toxic mercury contained inside the tube. This creates a problem if you drop and break one on the carpet at home, thinking that it can be 'hoovered' up with your vacuum cleaner. Because what happens is, the toxic dust is sucked up and blown back out into the room in minute particles, that can then be easily breathed in without noticing. Can you imagine how many people, who, unaware of the dangers, would actually go to all the trouble of recycling their old fluorescent lamps? As an Electrician, I would have to take them away and pay to have them recycled, and then pass that cost on to the customer! Most customers, at that point, then decide to dispose of them themselves. I wonder if, in their infinite wisdom, the European Union, in the name of climate change, has given proper consideration to the banning of traditional light bulbs.

Because with total disregard for people's right to choose, and absolutely no concern for the terrible impact this will have on those with light-sensitive health conditions, who suffer from the emission of ultraviolet and the blue part of the visible spectrum, (tests by the Health

Protection Agency have shown that the new compact fluorescent bulbs (CFL's) emit both) are potentially putting their health at risk. It's strange isn't it, how, through EU directives, we have been bullied in to accepting undemocratic EU law without ever being asked. It's true that we elect MEP's but they don't make the laws and have no power to change or veto legislation passed by the unelected commission. We have been told by our masters that we must use energy saving light bulbs so as to reduce our carbon footprint, but have you noticed how many office buildings and motorways burn lights all night long with a not a soul in sight? When I was young, all the lamp posts were switched off after bedtime, and if you looked up to the sky you could see the stars instead of an orange glow and permanent 'daylight'.

*

Uniform was compulsory (although the cap had been cast-off long ago) in senior school, and ours was black blazer, grey flannels (no stay-press then) and a black and white striped tie, and of course black leather shoes, that not to polish every day was frowned upon by the games master, Mr Hurn. Sounds more like an army training camp doesn't it? Despite all the rumours, it was a good school.

There were four 'Houses' Auckland, Ottawa, Melbourne and Kingston, with house meetings two mornings a week after assembly. Assemblies took place every morning, where we were told to stand, as the Headmaster entered the hall and walked down the central aisle, wearing a cape and mortar-board, with a bible under his arm. We only sat down again, when invited to do so, once he was in position at the lectern upon the stage.

He would explain how the school took its name from a 17th century Quaker (1644-1718) who, born during the reign of King Charles 1, grew up during the rule of Oliver Cromwell and was buried in a small burial ground not far from here in the Quaker meeting house in the village of Jordans, Buckinghamshire.

He would read from the bible, give us moral advice and teach us Christian values. Then, along with Mr Hamlin the Geography teacher, on the piano, we'd sing two or three popular hymns, like 'To be a Pilgrim' and 'Onward Christian Soldiers' and always say 'The Lord's Prayer'.

Our Father Who Art In Heaven,
Hallowed Be Thy Name.
Thy Kingdom Come,
Thy Will Be Done
On Earth As It Is In Heaven.
Give Us This Day Our Daily Bread;
And Forgive Us Our Trespasses,
As We Forgive Those Who
Trespass Against Us;
And Lead Us Not Into Temptation,
But Deliver Us From Evil.
For Thine Is The Kingdom, The Power
And The Glory, For Ever And Ever.
Amen.

I can't imagine these sorts of assemblies taking place in state schools today, can you? What a shame!

*

The last holiday arranged by the welfare department, for me and my brother Jim, was to be two weeks in Western-Super-Mare at the Rotary Boys House. We were taken to Slough station and put on an express steam train to Western-Super-Mare, but first, we had to stop at Reading to pick up a group of about 25 to 30 boys who had come down from the Midlands. Once that was done and we were on our way again the boys all gathered around me and Jim and bombarded us with questions about London. I suppose to them, it was their important Capital City and they wanted to find out as much as they could about it.

We made one more stop about half way for refreshments and to stretch our legs, then continued on. The place we were to stay in was a large Victorian house, in South Road, at the top of the hill which we walked up and down at least twice a day. It was fully staffed with its own kitchen and large dining hall which provided us with three cooked meals a day that we were very glad of after all the activity and fresh sea air. There were washrooms, shower rooms and bathrooms, a music study, a sports hall and tennis courts. In the entrance hall was a large gallery staircase leading upstairs to the spotless 'Spartan' bedrooms, each of which contained eight beds to a room, made up with blankets, and crisp white linen sheets and pillow cases.

My best friend there was a boy called Ivor Differ from Bilston in Staffordshire. He played the piano in the evenings while a group of us sang along and that was jolly good fun. One night a week, we were allowed into a room that had a huge model railway which filled the entire room, with a dozen electric trains, that we could use under the supervision of Mr Hibbert, the house master. We had plenty of free time to go off exploring in the woods, but went mostly to the seafront, Saturday morning pictures and Church on Sundays.

*

Back at school, what the boys found most uncomfortable were the regular health checks. We were usually informed in advance of the nurse's visit. She would either be inspecting hair, teeth, and feet, or giving jabs for one thing or another; not all at the same time mind, but over the course of the year. The kids used to get very nervous, and drop off like flies with all sorts of excuses, to get out of it, but if you were in school it was almost impossible to escape. So the best idea I had of dealing with it was, to accept as soon as possible that it was inevitable, then mentally prepare and endure! That's easier said than done.

It was in my second year that we were told to prepare over the next two weeks to be vaccinated. Those who went first told the others how awful the jabs were, and showed us the marks and the swellings. Now, if I'd have had mine in the first tranche, I'd have been fine, but our class wasn't to be done until half way through the second week; probably Tuesday or Wednesday, which gave me too much time to think about it.

I nervously walked to school on Tuesday morning ready to take my turn, but once in school nothing was mentioned. All day long we waited in anticipation, some more confident than others, still we didn't receive the call; it wasn't fair, didn't they know what the agony of the wait was doing to us, or didn't they care? Wednesday morning, it had to be today! Mr Johnson told us Tuesday or Wednesday. I bet he was enjoying watching us squirm; with that smirk on his face. He was a bit like that you know; mean; a bit of a bully. He was the type that had complete control; not what I'd call a control-freak though but more of a disciplinarian, and he treated everyone the same. There were no favourites, you either got on with it, or kept out of the way if possible. Mr Johnson was my form teacher for three years, and I hated it. He was also the metalwork teacher, but fortunately, at the beginning of secondary school

I chose Woodwork, under Mr Mills, who I found much more agreeable.

Mr Johnson was a tough Yorkshire man, but fair. In the form room at registration he expected complete obedience from his pupils; if anyone at the back was talking or not paying attention, you'd see the blackboard rubber or pieces of chalk being hurled towards the offending article. Great entertainment that was, especially when that 'article' was called to the front of the class for punishment, which, in class was usually the 'slipper' or a rap across the knuckles with a ruler.

On one particular occasion, Allan Deverill happened to be the offending article during 'Technical drawing'; the class, which Johnson was taking that day, and the only correction-tool at hand was a T-square which was smartly applied across Deverill's back-side, breaking into several pieces on contact. No malice was borne against Johnson; we just thought that he was a natural bastard, and in the Metalwork shop on more than one occasion it would kick off between Johnson and one of the bigger older boys, but afterwards that would be the end of it.

Today, if a teacher can't keep discipline in his classroom he is lost and is unable to get on with his job. He ends up screaming at, and threatening the pupils who have set him up to be recorded on their mobile phones, which is then sent around the school, as well as being posted on 'You tube'. Great! The mob rule, or rather the 'pupils' in this case.

Before the ban on corporal punishment, which in almost every instance was dealt with in the classroom, 'nipped in the bud' so to speak, bad behaviour was prevented from escalating into an out-of-control situation, although there was always a joker that would try to push his luck. Dave Carter was one of these.

Now, Dave wasn't a bad boy, although, in the German room one day he decided to have some fun with Mr (Nobby) Clarke, otherwise known as 'Yogi Bear'. I don't know why they called him that because I thought he looked more like 'Fred Flintstone'. Anyway, Dave began to cause some disruption over something, bringing the lesson to a halt.

Goading 'Yogi', who continually asked him to stop, made for an entertaining spectacle. Dave was never going to go so far as to be expelled from the classroom, and his antics did provide fun for all. 'Yogi' knew this and decided to play along with it for a while when at a predestined time provided us with a grand finale by producing a size 10 'slipper' from which there was to be no escape. Dave leapt from his seat and hopped around the desks towards the back of the class.

'What is it to be Carter?' he asked, 'lines, or the slipper? 'Lines sir, 'haw haw haw!' he replied, where Yogi began counting the lines on the sole of the slipper. Come to the front Carter! 'aa'ah sir'rr' Carter complained, but it did him no good at all. 'Over the desk boy' whack! whack! whack! 'YAROOH' he howled, in true Bunter fashion, after every stroke, purely for the delight of his audience. The rotter! He gasped, as he returned to his seat (if you'll pardon the pun).

Anyway, I digress, back to the story about the jabs. It was now Wednesday morning, on the way to school, and with the same fear and apprehension. Today was the day! I'd built myself up so much by now, that the easiest thing to do, would be to stop thinking about it and just do it, after all it was only a couple of jabs and I'd probably have no side effects in any case. It's just amazing how a small thing like that can become magnified out of proportion just by dwelling on it.

As I'm nearing school all these thoughts are going round in my head. I could see the school gates in the distance, about a quarter of a mile away. When, wait! There is another way. I could take the day off sick and go in tomorrow with a forged sick note, all the other kids have done it; it never fails!? There that's the answer. Easy! Thursday morning and I haven't seen anyone from my class. What if they didn't have the jabs yesterday! I'd take today and Friday off and go in on Monday.

Well I didn't go back in on Monday the following week, or the week after that. The situation was now out of control, how was I going to get back into school? It was hopeless. How could I have let it go so far? It's a wonder Mr Whatmore the 'Wag' officer hadn't been called in. What to do? I've got to take a chance and go in with a 'note' I'll write that I've been ill with the Flu! It's perfectly reasonable to have two weeks off with Flu. That settles it then. I knew my mum's handwriting and started on the forged sick note, signed: Mrs Wight. No envelope necessary, just hand it in, that's all we'd ever done before.

We're lined up outside class waiting for Mr Johnson to let us in. It feels as if I haven't been at school for an age; all my class mates are asking me questions and want to know where I've been, which was only drawing attention towards me. I wish they'd all just be quiet. Johnson soon arrives to unlock the door and we file in, I positioned myself somewhere in the middle of the queue so as to appear inconspicuous.

Johnson is scrutinising each child as they pass by. As I get closer, note in hand, I take a deep breath, calm myself and give him it saying: 'sorry I've been absent Sir, but I've been ill'. 'In you go' he says, with a smile on his face. Actually he always had a smile on his face, he was probably quite a nice bloke really, and I don't ever remember him losing his temper.

We all take our seats, he calls the register, and that's that; I'm back in, and it feels great, but wait! Why is he thumbing through the pages of the register? He takes out another sick note and is comparing it with mine; what is he doing? My stomach begins to churn over and I'm sweating. You could hear a pin drop.

'Wight, come here!' he requests. 'Yes sir', say's I; showing me the sick note, he asks: 'who wrote this note?' 'My mum sir' say's I. He then produces the second note and asks: 'then whose is this one?' I nearly died as he held the two notes up to show me, both apparently written by my mum, but both clearly written in a different hand.

'Which one of these did you write?' he challenged. What! How could he know? I decided to end it right there and come clean. Pointing at the forgery, 'that one sir' I said, shamefully. I didn't care now; it was over. Or was it? "Go to the secretary, Mrs Douglas, for the 'cane and the punishment book and stand under the clock'" he commanded. That was the place pupils were sent to for any impending punishment. It was 'under the clock' in the corridor, outside the hall opposite the Headmaster's study. So if you were there, everyone knew what for. I missed the House meeting, because I had to stand there in isolation for forty minutes until the bell for the first class was sounded. A crowd of my friends and school mates soon gathered around to support me, knowing what was to come. 'It'll be alright, don't worry' they said reassuringly.

Johnson appeared, walking down the centre of the corridor, and as he drew close the small crowd separated forming a semi-circle around me. As I handed him the cane he told me to touch my toes and straighten my knees. He took two steps back, then there was a swish and 'Whack' that nearly sent me over; I then immediately began to bawl, I was only 4ft nothing, just a little kid. Two or three of the older boys put their arms around me to take me away, saying to Johnson: 'that's enough Sir' to which he said: 'I haven't finished yet, put him back'.

Same again, bend over; swish 'Whack' this time the cane broke and I heard the pieces roll across the floor; Wah! That air of confidence, that half smile; his demeanour unchanged throughout. He hands me back the cane and punishment book and walks back the way he came. It was over now, thank God. I could now just blend in and get back to normal. I don't blame Johnson for caning me, it was my own fault, and I'd brought it all on myself. My mum knew nothing of it and probably didn't want to, and that was best all round.

Initially, I found the transition to secondary school quite tough, especially because it was an all-boy's school with all male teachers, I much preferred the mixed learning environment of Godolphin. Suffice it to say, it took me a while to settle in; although, I had lots of friends there, and my 1st year form teacher Mr Mills was very kind. He would read to us, stories such as 'the monkey's paw' and 'Ants'. He had a great reading voice and always left us wanting more.

My choice of workshop was woodwork and coincidently, the woodwork Master was Mr Mills. I enjoyed that class very much.

During the 3rd year we were assigned to design and make something, so I chose to make a bedside cabinet. It was nothing special, just a box-shaped dual compartment with shelves and doors, on legs. It was whilst in the science lab, a few days later that, thinking I was in trouble, Mr Mills called me out of class into the corridor and began praising me for this design. I couldn't believe it! Here I was in this, what I thought 'hostile' environment gaining recognition and encouragement from one of the masters. From that day on everything changed.

A week or so later a Prefect fetched me from the playground to 'stand under the clock'; that could only mean one thing; the whack! I'd stood under that clock several times in the early days, in what I called my unsettled period, and on one occasion received the maximum punishment; Six o the Best! Two strokes on each hand, and two on the backside, but instead of awaiting punishment, I was taken in to the office by the secretary, to where the Headmaster and his deputy were standing beside his desk.

He had an eager, kind, fatherly composure and began talking to me in a normal fashion that showed he was genuinely concerned for his pupils. Somehow, he seemed to know a lot about my background; how I came from a large family that was very poor, and so arranged for me to go on a residential trip to Snowdonia National Park, which included all types of outdoor activities, 'Great fun! and all tremendous experiences for a young teenager.

My time at school continued in this positive way and I enjoyed it very much never missing a day. I even volunteered to go back in the evenings three times a week for such things as canoe building. The evenings were run as a sort of youth club with time to relax and listen to music. I settled in very well and had many friends, some of whom I still see to this day. Some pour scorn on corporal punishment these days, but back then it was how they controlled bad behaviour and maintained discipline, and I hasten to add that it wasn't used as frequently as most people imagine but it was an effective deterrent.

As you can see from my experience, effort was encouraged and hugely rewarded. I would say that that makes for a happy and rounded existence for all concerned; teachers, parents and especially children, although, they wouldn't realise it until much later on in life.

The canoe building was in preparation for a forthcoming expedition on the River Wye, for a dozen or so pupils. It was to start in Hereford, and finish at Symonds Yat, just by the rope bridge near to the Lodge, which at that time was under construction. My friend and class mate Robert long was my partner for that week, in a two-man canoe, Mr Johnson and Mr Neuf were in charge, and Jeff Webb an ex-pupil was assisting. The Beatles were in the charts with their double 'A side' Strawberry fields and Penny Lane (1967) and every time I hear either of those two songs, it takes me right back to me and Bob 'shooting the rapids' at Symonds Yat, or carrying our canoe between rivers, overland. Portaging, Johnson used to call it.

We carried all our equipment with us, inside the canoes; that was, our tent, food, and cooking utensils etc, as well as clothing and sleeping bags. Can you imagine the weight? I wonder where Bob is, or if he's still in Slough somewhere – Bob, do you remember that Pub called 'The Bunch of Carrots?

Jeff Webb had left school several years earlier but came back to help with the canoes and, consequently, was invited to assist on the trip. Jeff and his family were well known and respected locally; his father had his own coal delivery service, and Jeff, by this time was a police cadet.

On the expedition we'd canoe all day, and then find a suitable place alongside the river to make camp over night. Everything had to be hauled up on to the bank and unpacked; the tents pitched, and the fire lit. After our meal the teachers would disappear down to the local pub, whilst we built up the fire, then sat around it singing and telling stories. Jeff and a couple of older boys kept an eye on us, so we were quite safe.

It was not until I was about 21 that I met Jeff again. Now, I've got nothing against coppers, but what he did beggars belief. It was while I was working up at Booker Airpark that, one lunch time, I had to go into Wycombe to pick up my wages from the office there. As I drove around the back to park, I noticed a Police car with two officers inside following close behind, when I got out I saw that one of them was Jeff Webb.

I was relieved and happy to see him, thinking that it had been a long time since we last spoke, but he hadn't stopped me for a friendly chat, in fact he began questioning me. Did I own the car? Why was I behind the shops? Etc, etc. Then he told me to stand aside and began pulling the seats out and emptying all the ash trays. At this point I thought that he was going way over the top, so I said 'Jeff! What are you doing'? To which he replied 'looking for drugs' but, I said 'I don't even smoke, and I've only got half an hour for dinner'. Both he and his pal stopped what they were doing, paused for a while, looked at me and said 'off you go then'.

Not only did I have no time to eat, but was puzzled and upset; even more so because, there was no apology from him, nor any recognition of our past friendship! In contrast to Jeff Webb's (and an old Pennanian at that) appalling behaviour and attitude towards me, an innocent member of the public, Johnson surprised us.

He kindly let those in his form, take their canoes home for the entire school summer holidays, to be used on the lake at Black Park, and he even came there to visit us with his wife and young children. How cool is that? Good old Sir!

These days I wonder how my son would have got on if he had been brought up in that era. No mobile phones, no computers or X-boxes; only three TV channels in black and white that finished at 10.30pm. I personally think he'd have made the most of it; there was so much more to do, especially in making your own fun.

We spent very little time in the house, preferring to be out and about with: 'be back before dark!' ringing in our ears as we ventured off.

One of the highlights of the year was when the Roses Fair came to Granville playing field in Manor Park, the centre of town. After watching all the 'cowboy' films with their six-guns and Winchester rifles, the shooting galleries became a great attraction. Whether live 22 or air guns, it was the closest we could get to the Wild West.

The Whip, the Big-wheel and the Octopus were my favourite rides, and still are, but modern fairgrounds don't have them anymore, and, in any case, don't seem that well attended these days. Having said that, Carters Steam Fair who tour the local area, have acquired most of the old rides that add to their collection, including other such attractions as: the 'Wall of Death' the 'Rotor' and the steam-powered 'Swing-boat' to name but a few, which people queue up for. That says something doesn't it? They have retained a popular, proven formula that still draws in the crowds today! And what music do they play? the popular, unbeatable tunes of the 1950's and 60's.

Fairgrounds and rock music to me are a classic combination, like strawberries and cream or Lennon and McCartney.

I am so glad that I grew up when I did. The music of the 1960's, to me, was the best ever; spawned in, and inspired by the revolutionary rock and roll era of the late 1950's. I love the Beatles music and am so happy that I was there when they burst on to the music scene, and stayed there during my teenage years. In fact, that whole era was filled with great new sounds; the Rolling Stones for one, plus many more.

In 1970, I had the opportunity to go to Liverpool and visit the Cavern club where the Beatles used to play and Cilla Black used to work. I was there to witness the whole area being bulldozed. In fact, the Cavern club was the only solitary building of the block still standing. I didn't return again to Liverpool until just recently, this time with my son, who was training there with the KUGB (Karate) England squad. This gave me a great opportunity to tour this magnificent city, which included a visit to John Lennon's (Mendip's), and Paul McCartney's house in Forthlin Road; Penny Lane, Strawberry Field, etc. which were all incorporated in the 'Magical Mystery Tour'. It was then suggested that we visit the Cavern Club afterwards, at our leisure, for refreshments.

The original Cavern club closed in March 1973 and was filled in during construction work on the Mersey-rail underground rail loop. It was rebuilt using many of the original bricks, to the original plans and at the same address, 10 Mathew Street, and re-opened on the 26th April 1984. Please, please, all you music lovers; go to Liverpool and discover the 'Mersey-beat' trail for yourselves; you won't be disappointed.

So there we sat sipping our drinks, in front of the stage, surrounded by 'Beatles' memorabilia, looking at a large picture on the wall, of the 'Fab Four'. I was telling my son all about how the Beatles and the 'Mersey-scene' had influenced the Pop era and my teenage years. 'I loved the Beatles music; they were actually here!' I told him. I was totally immersed in the aura of this atmospheric, iconic music venue; eyes glazing over, telling my son: 'THIS IS MY LIFE' when all of a sudden and without warning, the glass on my table exploded with such a crash that everyone seated around us, turned to see what the commotion was about. I just sat there stunned for a moment, listening to the Beatles music in the background, and then looked up to see a large picture of John Lennon smiling down on me.

We sat for a while and then made our way up the stairs and into the street. At that moment, I was totally immersed in the 'Mersey-sound' and in awe of the whole experience. We stood outside to pause for a while to take it all in, when there across the street was John Lennon himself, leaning up against the wall with his hands in his pockets (well, a statue at least) and by the side of us was a large poster of John Lennon with captions 'IN MY LIFE' advertising Mark McGann playing the role of John Lennon as he has been doing for over 30 years. I'll leave you to make of that what you will.

Mark McGann's first portrayal of John Lennon was at the Everyman Theatre in Liverpool, in 1981, just months after he was assassinated. When recently asked what his memories were of the time he said: "Much of it was a blur as you might imagine! I do though remember the incredible euphoric release at the end of the press night. The thought of it still makes the hairs stand up on the back of my neck. It was like a mass outpouring of grief, gratitude and a sense that something extraordinary had just taken place".

The Beatles and the Rolling Stones pretty much dominated the charts, with sometimes as many as five or six songs between them in the top ten. Other contemporary artists included groups such as The Seekers, The Kinks, the Who and the Tremoloes. And among the soloists were: Roger Whittaker, Petula Clark, Gene Pitney, Cilla Black, and Mary Hopkin best known for her 1968 UK number one single "Those Were the Days". She was one of the first musicians to sign to The Beatles' Apple label.

The 1960's music was vast and varied, with Rock bands, such as Led Zeppelin. 'Folk', and singer song writers, Donovan, (Britain's answer to Bob Dylan) and very good he was too, (He was one my friend Jimmy Birkett's favourites; do you remember Jim from my first day at school?) and Cat Stevens, all vying for a place in the charts with their particular brand of music.

When I bought my first pop record for about 4/- (20p) in 1964; it was 'Diane' by the Bachelors. Incredibly, the Bachelors put more records into the UK top ten than The Beatles in that year with Diane reaching number one.

Now, I know that you will all have your own personal favourites; there was such a variety to choose from, but you have to admit don't you? That it was a great time for music!

At the age of about 13 the Council decided that we should have a bigger house; I wondered what took them so long. I suppose that it was because our family comprised two young teenage boys with three older sisters still living at home. Waterbeach Road, two streets away was where they sent us, not far away, just around the corner really. 104, was a nice double-fronted four bed roomed house with an indoor toilet, and a parlour.

Me and Jimmy had one of the back bedrooms, that overlooked Granville Park which was very nice to play in, was convenient as a short cut to the Farnham Road and also for school and held the Fairground each year, right on the doorstep, great wasn't it! I loved that house; there was so much space inside and out, and it had an Air raid shelter in the back garden that made a very useful coal-bunker.

Jim Mum Me

The new house, being so close by, didn't present us with any problems usually associated with that sort of upheaval at such a young age, in fact it was a delight; a God-send. A lot of my school mates lived near to us. Monty lived opposite, Lenny Gales three doors away, Wynford Thomas, Christopher Watson, Alan Edison and many more (sorry to those of you that I've missed out) in the next street, and of course my next door meighbour Johnny Byrne. John wanted to go to William Penn but his mother sent him to St. Joseph's which upset him slightly, but not for long though, once he found out there were lots of girls there. John, who I see occasionally, has remained in Slough, and it is always a pleasure to meet him for a drink and a chat. In fact when we spoke recently, he told me that he meets up with Charlie Smith, who has since moved far away; every year Charlie was with us on a school educational trip to Snowdonia. "Having fun!" Charlie; on the dry ski slope, remember? Philip (Woggles) Watkins and Ronnie Poole were in my group.

John also reminded me of the sheep that Jackie Gibson used to keep in his front garden; who could forget that! These people were real characters!

Kenny Back and Jackie Gibson, who also went to William Penn, were mates and a year or two older than us, but nevertheless, we were all friends and neighbours.

Whilst on the way to the pictures one afternoon, me and my brother Jim met Kenny in Waterbeach Road approaching us. He'd called for Jackie but he wasn't in, and so asked if he could come with us, we didn't mind; the more the merrier. Well it all worked out quite well in the end, as I'll explain. Firstly, the film we were going to see was the new Clint Eastwood western, 'A Fistful of Dollars' and being under age we would need an adult to take us in. In these cases, kids would wait outside the picture-house until an adult agreed to accompany them and then disappear once inside. Secondly, you were less likely to get picked on if you were with someone older.

Anyway, so far so good; we settled into our seats, near the back, and began to watch the film when some nasty piece of work turned around to pick on the kids sitting next to us, who meekly shrank back down into their seats, he then roared at us, saying we best do the same or else! Nasty Fxxxer; with this, Kenny stood up, towering above us and said; "I don't like being spoken to like that", and "pick on someone your own size"! The aggressor then sank back down into his seat, fuming, with steam coming out of his ears. Me and Jim looked at each other and chuckled. "That'll make him teach" said little Jim.

*

There is often talk of arming the Police, there are also views for and against. More importantly, the thing that most people agree on, is that there should be a high visibility Police presence on the street, i.e. more Bobbies on the Beat! The English Bobby is respected all over the world for his honourable and considerate professionalism. He is praised in amazement by foreigners, at his ability to do his job efficiently, unarmed!

Unfortunately though, we no longer see Police constables out tackling crime on the street anymore. I believe that, regardless of what they keep saying about modern policing methods, a Policeman on the street can see more of what's going on in the neighbourhood, get to know the locals, who are only too keen to speak to him, and in that way find out who the villains are.

The public feel safe and love to see a copper in uniform pounding the Beat; it gives them a sense of security. It's effective too, in stamping out anti-social behaviour; spitting, swearing and shouting in public, throwing down litter and so on. There is, in my opinion, no substitute for a Bobby on the Beat. Not only are they there to protect the general public from hooligans, but are very effective at reducing crime by nipping it in the bud, purely due to their constant presence in the neighbourhood, to the extreme annoyance of the would-be criminal. Let me give you an example from my own personal experience.

It was about 7 o'clock in the evening and dark, while me and my friend John Clifford, at the age of around 15 were standing outside the Ambassador Picture house talking to some girls, when a young copper approached us on a bike. He was smiling and friendly and just wanted to get to know us, and was keen to have any information about his new beat as he'd only been assigned that week.

As we told him our names and addresses, and what school we went to, a single car pulled up a couple of hundred yards away on the other side of the Farnham road (a dual carriageway), outside the Chemist, two or three of the men jumped out and one of them chucked a brick through the window, shattering the whole pane; the copper shouted at them as they were about to take goods from the window display. If what happened next you'd seen in a film, you would not believe plausible in real life.

The copper put away his notebook and pencil, ran with his bicycle, hopped with one foot onto the pedal, threw his other leg over and gave chase, pedalling from a standing position, closing the gap rapidly. The crooks screeched off down Furnival Avenue empty handed with this policeman in hot pursuit. They must have been terrified! Because this copper meant business! But seriously though, a police presence on the street does make a difference.

A Beat Bobbie's job is to remain vigilant, take notes and ask questions, and act on or pass that information on to his superiors; he is, in all probability, our first line of defence.

When I was about 18, I was walking down the Farnham Road on the way home from seeing my girlfriend. We'd been swimming during the day, but it was now 10.30pm, and I still had my trunks and towel rolled up under my arm when a Policeman emerged from one of the shop doorways. There was no one else in sight so I wasn't too surprised when he asked me to stop. I was a little confused though, when he asked me what I had under my arm; it was obvious what it was.

Anyway I unrolled the towel and showed him what was inside? He smiled and explained that, I could have been going out equipped to do a robbery, with tools concealed inside the rolled up towel. I was flabbergasted but admired his zeal. I didn't feel threatened, but instead, quite happy and confident that we all could sleep safe in our beds, knowing that this policeman and thousands like him throughout the country were conscientiously going about their Duty, unarmed!

John Clifford was in my form all the way through secondary school, and also my partner in woodwork, but in the last term of the 4th year I didn't see much of him. I know that he worked at a fruit and veg. shop on the Farnham Road in his spare time, and had indicated to me on a previous occasion that he wanted a job with a friend on the coal, and as there weren't many weeks remaining until we left school, I suspect that was what he was doing.

When he did show up, Johnson, our form teacher quizzed him about the coal round and added that it required great strength to haul 1cwt sacks of coal all day; I don't think he believed that John was strong enough to do it, and so, challenged him to an arm wrestle. Johnson used all his strength until he was red in the face, and he was no weakling himself, but failed to budge John's arm an inch as he held his position expressionless.

The last time I saw John he was working for Neville & Griffin as a Milkman.

The school leaving age back then was 15, some stayed on to do GCE's, most left and went into apprenticeship's then on to Technical College, but many, many more went into factories or shops. There was no shortage of work anywhere.

I already knew what I wanted to do, but wasn't quite sure how to go about it, so it was straight down to the Careers' Office to enrol for an apprenticeship as an Electrician.

At 15 I was just a kid, a Minor, and nothing could be done without the consent of my parents; so that was the end of that. My mum couldn't afford to keep me, or send me to college, and even if she could, it was usually the Fathers job to get his son into an apprenticeship, but mine wasn't around, so I had to give it up as a lost cause.

Can you imagine how disappointing that is for a child, old enough to go out to work and pay his way, but too young to take a life changing career decision? It was hopeless! It wasn't that there was no work or a shortage of jobs, it was quite the opposite; everyone had a job. There were no lavish benefits to be had, and if you signed on the Dole you were expected to attend the office every day or every other day, I'm not sure which.

It was considered to be shameful for the able-bodied to sign on for state handouts and you would quickly be singled out as a scrounger.

Which reminds me of the time back at school, staring out of the window, whilst standing at the English teacher's (Bob Beynon) desk as he checked my work, when I noticed one solitary man walking in the, otherwise, deserted street and wondered what he could possibly be doing or what he would do for money come the end of the week.

All manual workers were given a pay packet at the end of each week, and if they were able to save a little, it was usually put into a Post Office Savings account. Only professional people had bank accounts and cheque books. You were expected to behave yourself and work hard; National Assistance was for the genuine needy, not a career choice.

In the early 1980's a young girl that I hadn't seen for a while, walked past the house pushing a baby in a pram. Quite taken aback, I said: 'oh! I didn't know you were married' to which she replied: 'oh, I'm not married, I'm not even in a relationship; this is my passport to a council flat; I want my independence!'!

I would never have believed it, had it not come from the horse's mouth. But that was the start of things to come, wasn't it?

Work experience begins

Most kids wouldn't have been given pocket money so they took spare time jobs as a way of having their own spending money, and there was always plenty of work for school children, after all it was a good source of cheap labour. Whether it was Saturday jobs, a paper round, picking up litter at the Baylis Lido or helping roundsmen, there was always something useful to do; caddying at the golf course, pop bottling (10 @ 3d on each empty returned = 2/6 = the average weekly pocket money allowance) the list was endless.

Back then, you would hardly ever see a pop-bottle, can or rubbish anywhere. Pop bottles, for onc were money. Compare that to the time I returned from Japan in 1997 and decided to take a walk down memory-lane, through Salthill Park and beyond, to where I use to live and play; I couldn't believe the mess everywhere. Well most of Slough is looking like that these days.

My job was helping the Paraffin man deliver from door to door, from a Bedford TK lorry with a large tank on the back, using a hand pump to fill the cans.

The Paraffin lorry

Nobody that I knew had central heating, but instead of coal, the paraffin stove was quickly becoming a convenient alternative.

With new modern designs, the paraffin stove was attractive efficient and portable. No need for a coal bunker, setting a fire or clearing the ash pan, this was controllable heat at your fingertips. After all, this was the sixties; the age of innovation. Personally, though, I preferred the open fire and I still have one now, although not from necessity.

The paraffin stove, to my mind, was smelly and dangerous, especially around children; it needed a clear free space to stand in, and was very often the cause of many house fires. Nevertheless, it was the preferred method of keeping warm in the winter. There were very few cars in the streets then, but when I pass by the houses of the round these days, and see the amount of cars parked with two-wheels-up on both sides of the street, I realise that it would be impossible to do that job now.

Anyway, that was my job, we did do it, and it was good hard work. I was only twelve years old and quite small, but I could use the hand pump, and carry two full five gallon (25lts) drums; although, at only 4 foot nothing, and at full stretch, I managed to lift them a clear 2 inches off the ground and deliver them to the doors. Work started on a Friday night after school until 10pm for 10/- (50p) and all day Saturday for 10/- usually making about £3 in tips for both days.

There were a lot of West Indian families in Slough by now (1963) and the women were always kind to me, they'd give me sweets and money, and sometimes they would say: 'you hungry Ken neh, you want some food?' I was always hungry, so never turned down the offer.

	£	s	d	
1 Gallon of paraffin	0	2	4½	Equal to (11½p)
2		4	9	
3		7	1½	
4		9	6	
5		11	10½	

The money was collected at the door, or safely left under the cans, which invariably amounted to quite a few shillings sometimes, along with the change. Incredibly, it didn't occur to anyone to go in and steal it? This option of payment applied to the other trades as well, including the milkman.

We only worked in the winter months, street lighting was poor and it was cold and dark but I loved it. If it rained I wore a flat cap and a cape, I never felt the cold because the job was extremely physical and I became quite strong and tough for a little chap.

The highlight of a Friday night was when I delivered to Avrils's house in Northampton Avenue, she was about my age and I swear the best looking girl in the world, but I never got the chance or had the nerve to talk to her. It was heartbreaking!

When I returned home at 10pm my poor mum would open the door with a relieved look on her face, it must have been difficult for her. Each night I would hand over my wages, and keep my tips, she would have appreciated that.

For those not familiar with pre-decimal (Sterling) currency, the above chart may look a little complicated. But if you were taught this system throughout school, as I was, it's really very easy.

Pounds shillings and pence (£.s.d. or L s d) as it was known, had 12 pennies to the shilling (5p), and 20 shillings to the pound which remained that way until 15th February 1971.

You could have a ha'porth or three ha'pth (half penny worth) of something, or be a soppy ha'pth (a fool) – pronounced – ay'pth. You could also, of course, have six pennyworth of chips, which is what you paid then for a single portion of chips.

You could then put in your two-bobs worth – have your say. You could also go into John Collier, Jackson or Burtons Tailors &menswear, and buy a suit off the peg for around 50 bob (£2.50p). *"John Collier, John Collier the window to watch"*.

240 pennies to the pound had been in existence since Anglo-Saxon times; the shilling was later introduced in 1548 by Henry VIII. The 5p and 10p were circulated in 1968 to replace the one and two shilling piece respectively; they were the same size and weight, probably to wean us off our ancient and preferred currency.

One of the reasons I heard for decimalisation was the fact that foreigners couldn't understand it, but we all know the real reason now don't we? It was to pave the way for the single currency (Euro) necessary for European political union. Exactly one year later Prime Minister Edward Heath, saying, 'there will be no loss of essential sovereignty', signed the first of the five European treaties culminating in the Lisbon Treaty, which effectively handed over huge swathes of powers to make our own laws to a foreign country, therefore surrendering our sovereignty without a fight or democratic mandate.

There are those that say that decimal money is easier to use and that units of 10 are simpler, you don't have need too much brainpower, but that to me sounds like dumbing-down. So instead of raising standards to increase academic excellence, should we lower the bar to allow under achievers a more level playing field? Why stop there? We could, for example, introduce a 10 hour clock, or have 10 months in a year? I can't see how it would work though, because it would go against nature. We still have road signs in 'miles' and we still measure our height in feet and inches, but we can't continue with a dual system of measurement and be fully integrated into the EU, everything must be harmonised.

At school we were taught that in an electrical circuit: Red = positive (live) and Black = negative (neutral). EU directives for harmonising colours of electrical circuits, now says that Brown and Blue are standard cable colours for British domestic wiring (Single Phase) Confusing? It gets worse. Commercial and Industrial colours (Three Phase) that used to be very clear and unmistakably Red, Yellow, and Blue are now Brown, Grey and Black. You try to distinguish those colours in subdued light or when the fuses have blown, for example. It's just another classic case of EU meddling into every aspect of our daily life.

When I think back to those days I find it remarkable now that most of the men had been in the Second World War, the 'Paraffin man had been a sergeant in the army. My friend Harold's Dad, Ralph had fought in the Middle East and Italy, and Alan's Dad, Reg had been in submarines; my own dad was only 19 when with the expeditionary force in Dunkirk.

Likewise, many of our customers and people I have met while growing up had been tank commanders, crew members of Lancaster or Wellington Bombers, or had served in Burma (the forgotten army) etc.

I personally have met and heard of the exploits of two ex Japanese POWs. And had been brought up on war films like 'The longest Day', 'The Great Escape', 'The Heroes of Telemark' and the myriad of Black and White films out of the Ealing studios, it was just a normal part of life. Those men in their 40's and 50's were living history. Legends! Heroes!

Life after school

It was 1967 when I left school with no qualifications and no chance of getting into College, so reluctantly, I had to accept my lot and limitations, but either way, I had to get a job. There would be no lying in bed or lounging about the house all day, it was out at 8am and back at 5pm and I was expected to pay my way come Friday teatime. It sounds harsh doesn't it? But at the time, there were still four of us at home plus my mum, and the bills had to be paid.

Luckily, my brother-in-law found me a job working with him in the Foundry. It was a bit of a shock though, to go from the classroom into a noisy, smelly, dirty Fettling shop starting with the most menial of tasks. The foreman sat me at a desk that had a hand-operated punch on it, gave me a box of castings that I had to pass through it separating the pieces; try to imagine it, it was like knocking out the teeth of a comb. After 2 hours of that a bell sounded, everyone turned off their machines and started walking out, but I didn't realise that it was the 10 o'clock tea break, because no one had told me, so I carried on until one of the men came back to get me. He led me to a small room where some other boys sat on chairs eating their sandwiches. After 15 minutes, another bell sounded to bring us back to work; I looked into my box and noticed that I'd almost completed my first task, so I signalled (because you couldn't hear yourself think) to the foreman to come over, he said; 'well done!' took the empty box away and came back a minute later with another full one; and so that procedure carried on all day. I went to work in the morning clean and smart, and came home in the evening filthy; it was diabolical and I hated it. They'd give me different jobs, moving me from one bench to another, but really it was all the same sort of thing. I was so bored, that I'd daydream I was still at school with all my friends, and in any case it was the school summer break, so I'd have been at the pool or out all day having fun.

The best part of the job was payday, which was on a Friday and the end of the working week. Hooray! I'd buy a new record every week. The Beatles had been quiet for a while, then they announced the release of their next album which was to be called 'Sgt. Pepper's'; well, it was brilliant and a huge success. Later I replaced the LP vinyl and bought it on CD, which I still regularly play. My 16 year old son, who is still at school, has an MP3 player, an I-pod, a 'Blackberry' Smartphone with internet connection, on contract, an HD TV, a play station, an X-box, and X-box live which enables him to play on-line with his friends; Oh!, and a lap-top. When I was his age I had been in full time employment for a year, taught myself to play the harmonica and guitar, and with my own money, bought a new 'Fidelity' portable radio for £12; my wages were £10 a week before deductions. Radio 1 was just a year old, the music was the best ever and I listened to it on my radio all the time, especially in the morning before work, with Tony Blackburn, while having breakfast.

Oh! Where was I? Oh yes, I remember…I'd get the bus at 7.30am but it never got to the Factory gate until 8 o'clock, I'd then have to run to clock-in and was always late; if it was anything over 8.03am they would deduct a quarter of an hour's pay. It was bloody awful! I suppose I could have got on the earlier bus and arrived at 7.30am, but I decided to buy a motorbike, a BSA C15 250cc instead, and go to work on that. One day after three months of that tedious torture, I was halfway to work, sitting on my bike at the traffic lights that seemed to be stuck on red for an age; it was a beautiful sunny Autumn morning, and it was as if time were standing still as I pondered the idea of whether to carry straight on to work, or turn left into town and go to our favourite café for a cup of tea and a fried breakfast. It was a glorious defiant moment that I revelled in; no longer was I that naïve child of 3 months ago but a 16 year old young man, a fully fledged school leaver. I was now an experienced full-time worker and confident that I could get a job anywhere.

The lights were still red, how long had it really been? I revved the engine, anxious to pull away, still undecided I looked up at the clear blue morning sky and felt the warmth of the sun over me; I was somewhere else. The lights changed, reality dawned and the factory beckoned, it was now or never; was I really mature or strong enough to break away? Amber, green. I slipped the bike into gear, opened the throttle and away; left into Chalvey Road East, across the lights into Albert Street then left towards the end of the High Street and Sid Moram's motorcycle shop where we used to go on a Saturday, then across the road to the café where we'd eat and drink and play records on the Juke-box.

We were the 2nd generation 'Rockers' dressed in studded leather jackets, gloves and boots, helmet and goggles, and riding our bikes in all weather. As I sat there finishing my tea I felt a great feeling of relief, I was in control, and although a trade was out of the question I was going to get a job that I wanted to do, so got back on my bike and headed off towards the Trading Estate. As I went across the Farnham Road and onto the estate via Edinburgh Avenue, I spotted Maxine Pinckney, a school friend standing by the 'Estates Railway' crossing; he had a start at 'Norstel Scaffolding' the first factory unit on the left, so I waited with him until his crew turned up.

He was a fellow 'Rocker' and 'old Pennanian' and we had a great chat about bikes, work and so on and the possibility of getting a start with him, but I didn't fancy scaffolding. Anyway that was how easy it was to get a job. As we stood there talking for about half an hour, a worker in overalls came out from the Rolex Paper Co next door so I asked him if there were any jobs vacant. With that he went back in and brought out the Stores foreman (Don Trivet) who offered me a job as a stores assistant for 5/- hour (£10 week) including free, clean overalls every Monday.

The job involved weighing rolls of (slit) paper, of which there were many different types, and taking it around the factory on a sack-barrow or forklift to the men on the machines, who made it into tubes of different sizes for packaging and so on. Working hours were 8am – 5pm with an hour for dinner in the subsidised canteen, with additional 15 minute tea breaks in the morning and afternoon. I'd made the right decision and landed on my feet; starting the following Monday. The job was literally on the doorstep and in familiar territory with the added bonus of, once starting; finding out that lots of people seemed to know me, including the Factory manager Mr Fred Stokoe, who knew my family, and what a nice man he was! I was free to move around the factory unhindered, and provided that we kept the machines supplied, the men were happy. The women worked at tables in a separate bay away from the big machines and their work was more intricate. It was such an absolutely, completely different and interesting working experience and environment that I could not believe my luck.

Between keeping the men working, there were Lorries bringing the huge rolls of paper from the local paper mills, that had to be unloaded at 'Goods In' by forklift truck, then stacked in their designated areas in the stores. Whilst at the other side of the factory in 'Despatch' there were Lorries to be loaded with the finished product. When the chap I was assisting left, the foreman gave me the store man's job until they could find someone older to do it. Quite a big responsibility for a 16 year old wouldn't you say? But it wasn't difficult, and I thoroughly enjoyed it.

Heading up towards Christmas, a "Firm's Dinner and Dance" was organised to take place in the Slough Town Supporters Club at the 'Dog Track', on the site of the Greyhound Stadium which also housed the football ground; the track ran round the pitch. I wasn't that keen on going, because I thought that it was a bit late to have dinner and I didn't dance! It also seemed to me that this sort of thing was for adults, and I was really still just a kid, but I was encouraged by the older ones, and was allowed to bring a friend. Me and my friend dressed up, wearing a shirt and tie for the occasion, and went to meet the coach, that was laid on, at the end of our street; a bit extravagant I thought when we could have walked it in 20 minutes. The restaurant was festively adorned with Christmas decorations and lights, and very nicely situated in the viewing lounge on the first floor, with the tables, set, next to huge glass windows overlooking a match that was going on.

This was a good idea after all! I was sat with my friend and all my workmates, all in party hats, having a great time, laughing and telling jokes. This was the first time in my life that I felt like an adult. When that was over me and my friend could have quite happily gone home; but 'the best part of the evening was yet to come'; we were told. So off we went to the dance hall on the ground floor. The music was playing 'loudly' it was almost dark inside and the people were flying about all over the place; my Foreman, Mr Trivet, normally of a quiet and responsible disposition, was the instigator of all this 'jollity' (Trivet - by name, and by nature, influenced by the Old English *thrifte*, three footed) was charging around in his party-hat like a man possessed; hooking up with the ladies on the dance-floor, first by his left arm, then by the right; on a mission; fixed gaze; tongue hanging out. What the bloody hell was he doing of? Dear old Don Trivet; a lovely man really, probably just letting his hair down, aided by a pint or two of amber liquid he said was apple juice? Looking back now, he was the life and soul of the party, but all the same, we weren't brave enough to venture in, spending the rest of the evening in the foyer.

The greyhound stadium was extremely popular and always well attended. When it first opened on Saturday 26th May 1928, it was only the second in Europe, attracting a crowd of over a 1,000 people. It was also a convenient location for the town's football ground, being situated near the town centre. Sadly, in 1973, Slough football club was relocated on the outskirts of town in Wexham, to a purpose built club on a green site provided by the council; which, in my opinion, was nowhere near as grand and exciting as their former home. For a start, it wasn't a stadium as such, but a single storey brick built clubhouse, with a flat roof by the side of a football pitch, but it served its purpose I suppose, even though it was a bit of a trek from the railway station in town, for visiting supporters.

Inevitably though, the writing was on the wall for the greyhound stadium because of its prime location and the prolific rise of the mega-store, which saw the site sold off to developers, who demolished everything on it in order to build a Co-op Superstore, which was always empty. I secretly believe that it was boycotted in protest over the closure of the dog-track. The last night of racing was held on Saturday 21st March, 1987. After which it was promptly closed, and bulldozed.

Another act of vandalism, I thought, was the sell-off of an equally similar prime-spot, adjacent to the railway station, which housed the 'Licensed Victualler's School'. That was demolished to make way for a new Tesco superstore, a mere quarter of a mile away from the Co-op, in the same road. Incidentally, while all this was going on I lived in central Slough, and saw all the High Street food shops close one by one, until it was only possible for me to shop, by driving to one of these stores by road. Very unsatisfactory! Still, that's progress as they say, isn't it?

In 2010 or there about, the old dog-track site was flattened again and a new building began to take shape in exactly the same style and lines as the old stadium. Many people, I expect, were speculating that two superstores almost next to each other was a bit of a planning oversight, and maybe, just maybe, the town planners had seen the error of their ways, and decided that we needed a sporting venue in the town after all. Well, low and behold as the new structure took shape, twice as high and as large as the previous one; the hoardings went up exclaiming: the forthcoming "opening of an exciting new Sainsbury's" whoopee!

Greyhound racing can still be attended at stadiums up and down the country but, regrettably, not in Slough anymore. It is still one of the country's most popular spectator sports, commanding huge crowds of around three million nationwide. They can cater for any occasion, whether it's for birthdays, anniversaries, retirement or Christmas parties. Whatever the requirement; family get-together or works outings; it's a great place to celebrate.

Back at work, on the day before the Christmas break, a party was held in the canteen for all the workers so we didn't do much work that day; and on New Year's Day, before it was declared a public holiday, only about 25 out of an approximate workforce of 200 turned in, so we didn't do much on that day either. In fact the Manager never turned up so we all went home early.

My BSA developed an engine fault, and rather than spending money on it, I sold it to one of my mates and bought my next bike, an Ariel Arrow 250cc, from one of the older boys at work, for £30. The 'Arrow' was a revolutionary design in Ariel's long motor cycle history, and years ahead of its contemporaries. The frame was of a pressed-steel construction, as opposed to the conventional tubular steel design of the period, which was hollow, very strong and light in weight, with the petrol tank under the seat. The conventional place for the petrol tank was a 'dummy' tank, for aesthetic purposes which contained a useful storage space. The unique design of the front forks, each comprising of a pair of trailing links with two-way hydraulic damping, gave a high standard of steering control and road handling, which added considerably to road safety and improved tyre wear. All of this, combined with a 250cc twin 2-stroke 'revvy' engine, with a top speed of 70mph, made for a completely different riding experience. That bike, new in 1960 was priced at around £150 including purchase tax. I went everywhere on that bike, but on one ride out, I learnt a very costly lesson. Many road users in those days would drive or ride illegally, but among my group, we all had insurance from Eversletts (about £15 a year), tax and an MOT from 'Tindal' in Duffield Lane. And what you avoided at all cost was the temptation to carry a pillion on a provisional licence. It was normal to have L-plates tied on but they didn't last very long and often came off. The Police only considered that a minor transgression and would usually pull you over for a 'Fatherly' chat about road safety.

So there I was, on my way to meet a fellow biker Lance Lennon in the High Street. Then just coming over the bridge in William Street and turning left towards the Station I saw Keith Sterry, one of my old class mates from William Penn, flagging me down. "Give us lift into Slough; it's only round the corner". I tried my best to resist but he was very persuasive. "Jump on then, quick... let's go". A couple of hundred yards down, we went, then right into Mackenzie Street and past Wellington Street on the left, when out of Curzon Street on the right came a Police car and pulled me up. "Is this your bike, etc. etc." he questioned. "Have you got a clean licence" he continued, "yes" I answered; "you won't have by the time I've finished with you" he said smarmily. He gave me a piece of paperwork and then Fxxxed Off. My mate was standing by the side of me, on the pavement, while all this was going on, and said "shall we go then?".

PC Savage was the Officers name. I went home and told my mum, I could now couldn't I? I was a young adult after all. My mum cursed him for being so nasty. Savage by name Savage by nature, she hissed! Why did he have to enjoy it so much? He'll get paid back for this; mark my words! A year later: *Slough Observer* reports: Police Officer suffers serious injuries after a head-on collision in Farthing Green Lane. PC Savage was speeding along a single-track lane and collided with a car coming the other way. Had he been wearing a seat belt he might have fared better, but the compulsory wearing of seat belts wasn't to come into force until 31st January 1983, a good 15 years later.

*

When I was at school I always had a push-bike, usually made up from several old bikes built into one good one, customised and painted with Woolworth's finest household gloss. My burning ambition though, was to have a motorbike as soon as I was old enough to ride one. It was the greatest thing to be out riding along country lanes, deliberately getting lost and discovering places otherwise too far to reach by pushbike. That was the case for me anyway, until one of my friends' Mum told us, that once, when she was younger she used to cycle from Slough to Guildford to work! What! That's even a long way to go to work by motorbike.

One day I set off on my bike to nowhere in particular and discovered Uxbridge. I was fascinated by its tube station and the old part of town around Windsor Street. It had a totally different atmosphere to most places I'd been to and I loved it. This was before it was modernised, when it still had its old Bus station and Police station. I remember that it had, at least, two beautiful old cinemas with grand foyers and staircases, and this is where I used to take my girlfriends for a run out on the bike. I saw 'Blackbeard's Ghost", 'The Italian Job' and 'Planet of the Apes' there, and just mentioning these jaunts now, brings back very pleasant memories. Before I move on from Uxbridge I would just like to mention that special place, the Tube Station. The first thing that catches your eye as you approach it from the High Street is the curved entrance and forecourt, with its little shops attached. Then, as you enter the ticket hall, there you see a row of telephone booths on the right hand side and the ticket office, with several windows, on the left. Further along, on the left is a café, beside which, are a few steps that take you outside to the bus station. All the furnishings were in dark wood; in that, I mean: the phone booths, the ticket windows, the doors and door-frames. It really had a pre-war feel about it. I thought it a very unusual and beautiful design. The café is still open and hasn't changed much; 'egg and chips, a slice of bread and butter and a cup of tea please'.

Having a 'Bike' though, wasn't just a means of transport to me, it was my identity; I was a 'Rocker'! I'd ride my bike everyday and everywhere a bit like a modern day Cowboy, and then one Saturday I met Mick Carpenter at the top of my road, while I waited to pull out as he passed by; he gave me a nod, as bikers do, and I pulled in behind until we reached the lights at the 'Goodies' and had a chat. He was out riding his bike doing exactly the same as me, so we decided right there and then to join up and go off together. It was much more fun to have a friend to ride with; we could stop at cafes and drink tea and chat. Yes, this was certainly much better. Just before we parted, later on in the afternoon, he asked me if I knew the 'Orchard Youth Club' which I did, but had never been; it was a 'bob' (5p) to get in and opened from 7.30 till 10pm weekday evenings. We agreed to go there together this coming Monday.

It was a great club, and very popular. Eventually, there was quite a group of us with bikes and at the end of the night we'd all start our bikes, warm them up a bit then race to the end of the long drive. I bet we were popular with the neighbours! Usually, because we didn't have to be in until 10.30pm we'd burn up the A4 to London airport (Later called Heathrow). The Orchard was where we socialised during the week; playing football, badminton, or table tennis whilst the Juke box played. It also had a small café, library and TV room but no one ever went in there. It's a shame there aren't any clubs like that now because we were never bored. The youth club leader and his wife would organise weekend educational trips to Aston Clinton in Buckinghamshire, or take us ice skating of a weekday night, on the mini bus to Richmond ice rink.

One of my favourite activities was to play the Pinball machine, which Jimmy Knox was the champion scorer. Jimmy was a little older than us, an ex-rocker who used to ride the iconic 650cc Twin carbed Triumph Bonneville; a real rocker, while we by comparison were just boys. Lois Manson was his girlfriend, and she was absolutely beautiful, we all fancied her something rotten, but they looked good together and made a handsome couple, who eventually married. They were both kind and friendly and would always talk or spend time with us. I also know, from Allan Deverill who met Jimmy just recently, that they are still happily married.

Although my job in Rolex was good, I didn't expect to spend the rest of my working life there; summer was approaching, the weather was becoming warmer, and as bikers we wanted to be out more. Mick Carpenter suggested that a trip down to the coast would be a good ride out for the coming Saturday, so we decided on Southsea. It was to be my first trip, and as Mick was a couple of years older than me he was going to take the lead, plus he had one of the fastest 250's in the South East. After a while we stopped to stretch our legs and have a rest, and Mick had this advice for me: 'most of the girls down the Coast like motorbikes, and boys in leather jackets, so be prepared!' Back on our bikes again we continued on, and stopped when we got to the first café along the way. No sooner had we ordered and sat down, than two of the prettiest young girls sat down beside us and didn't stop talking.

We arrived down in Southsea at about midday, parked up and had a wander round the funfair. I remember us going on the 'Cat and Mouse' and leaving our crash helmets on for safety's sake and because it looked cool! We were walking around enjoying ourselves when Mick spotted a tattooist, then on the spur of the moment decided that he wanted one. Whilst we were nervously hovering about outside, the man called us in. Not feeling very brave, Mick said to the man 'I don't really want one now, I'm just taking a look! Anyway does it hurt very much?' the man, seeing that Mick was a little apprehensive, sort of encouraged him by jokingly saying: 'well! I don't want to put you off, but last weekend, a strapping young sailor came in for a tattoo, and passed out half way through'. That broke the ice, so we had a laugh and began to look through the selection of tattoos on offer. Mick decided to have an eagle on his arm, but unfortunately, didn't have enough money to pay for it.

So I, being a good friend, lent him ten bob (50p) so that he wouldn't be disappointed. Back at the club, our adventure, and Mick's tattoo were the talking point of the evening, and the envy of all those not quite old enough yet to have a provisional licence.

We were well into the nice weather now and I was beginning to feel cooped up with working inside, so I decided that during the summer, I would like to work at a petrol garage as a pump attendant. This was before self-service petrol stations took over, after all I was experienced at working the pumps, and this would be a lot easier because they were electric, and there were no cans to be carried.

*

It had been announced in 1966 by the then Chancellor of the Exchequer, James Callaghan that decimal currency would be introduced in 1971. In 1968 the first two of the decimal coins, the 5p and the 10p came in to circulation (to run alongside sterling), were the same size and value as the 1/- and 2/- coins respectively, and co-existed until the early 1990's.

The old ha'penny (1/2d) was withdrawn in July 1969, the half crown (2/6d) followed in December; the 10/- note was replaced by the new 50p coin, although not withdrawn from circulation until November 1970. The old 1d (penny) and 3d (thruppence or threepenny piece) coins officially remained in circulation until August 1971. The idea of this gradual introduction, of the new decimal currency, was to familiarise the public with three of the six new coins, reducing the number to be introduced on D-day (decimal day). Because of the public outcry at the withdrawal of the sixpenny bit (6d) or Tanner, as it was affectionately called, its demise was postponed until June 1980.

Pre-decimal coins (sterling)		**Decimal in new pence**
Farthing	1/4d (denarius)	0.104p
Halfpenny	1/2d (Ha'penny)	0.208p
Penny	1d	0.417p
Three pence	3d (Threppenny bit)	1.25p
Sixpence	6d (Tanner)	2.5p
Shilling	1/- (a bob) or 1 shilling	5p
Florin	2/- (2 bob) or 2 shillings	10p
Half crown	2/6 (half a dollar) or 2 and a kick	12.5p
Crown	5/-	25p
Ten bob note	10/- (half a bar)	50p
£1 note	20/-	£1
Guinea	21/- (21 shillings)	£1.05p

Quite often of a Saturday night, a group of about half a dozen of us would walk into Slough, and meet up with others at the 'Brickmakers Arms', later to be renamed the Printers Devil, owing to the fact that the *Slough Observer* had just relocated there to a brand new purpose built print works opposite, and soon to become the home of the 'Old Pennanians' rugby club. The Club room had several Dart boards, a Bar-billiards table, a Juke-box and a friendly Landlord; although he did ask us to remove our leather jackets, and hang them up on the coat hooks. I didn't go there to drink, but for less than two bob (2/-) would order a hot steak and kidney pie and a glass of coke; we saw it more as an extension to the Youth club. I remember distinctly, the topic of conversation there one night, was of our concerns over all the talk in the news about the 'common market' and integration into all things 'European'. There was talk of having to drive on the 'right' hand side of the road; it was awful! Here we were, fledgling young men being told that everything we had learned at school was to be changed in favour of the European model. We were the English! Did all those people die in the war to protect our freedom and our sovereignty for nothing, only to have our politicians give it away without ever asking us, 'The People'?

*

Because my old school, William Penn was closed down in 1969, there were no more old Pennanians to carry on the tradition, and although the club still exists, it is now known as: the 'Farnham Royal (R.U.F.C.) Club' whose home is at Farnham Park Playing Fields.

The following picture was taken in the school gymnasium, is of the team that layed the clubs first ever game on September 15th 1962; courtesy of Dave Watson, himself an 'Old Pennanian' and currently the club vice chairman.

Mr Hurn Headmaster
The team that played the first ever game on the15th September 1962

On first contact with the club just recently, I spoke to the club president Richard Thomas and I can't tell you how delighted and happy I was to discover he was the same Richard Thomas that I was friends with when we were both 18, all those years ago. He had joined the 'Old Pennians' when he was about 19, and has been involved in the club ever since; more about Richard over the next few pages. We had a lot of catching up to do but also spoke about the success and longevity of the club who welcome supporters, young and old, as either playing or non-playing members, or even just casual observers. It is an old fashioned, friendly family orientated club where new players are warmly welcomed, whether experienced or complete beginners and everybody is entitled to a game as long as they give it their all.

In the early days, before the clubhouse was built, the team were based at the school where they used to change, walk the half a mile to the school playing fields to where the rugby pitches were situated, finish the game, walk back and have a shower. The members would then cycle into Slough, to the Brickmakers Arms, where they would enjoy a hot meal and an endless source of liquid refreshments.

I was devastated to find one day that my old school was being bulldozed. This was under New Labours policy to rebuild all the old schools as they were not deemed fit for modern day teaching methods!

I beg to differ. There was nothing wrong with the school; it was in perfect condition. I would suggest that the drop in standards since the 1960's had more to do with flawed government policy and 'trendy' modern teaching methods. On that site where once stood Senior, Junior, Infants and Nursery schools, in acres of its own land; there now stands a new school that resembles a pill-box, down in the bottom corner and a new housing development where my school once stood. So in reality, it was unnecessary to demolish my school unless it was always intended to be another 'land grab'. Shocking!

*

The youth club was a great place to be if you wanted information concerning the latest job vacancies, because it was full of youngsters like me trying to find their vocation in life. My job at the petrol garage would soon be coming to an end due to the change of usage and the redevelopment of that site, so that meant me looking for a new place to work. I discovered that 'Horlicks' had plenty of work and took on people regularly, so the next day I went to the factory's reception office to enquire. If you were to ever see the Horlicks factory you would have to agree that it is a magnificent Edwardian building. Set in its own land, next to the main railway line, with its close proximity to Slough Station, making it a highly visible historic landmark.

Nowadays there are high steel fences with spikes on top, closed gates and security guards surrounding the factory, but in 1968 it was just a matter of walking up to the front door and asking for a job, which is exactly what I did.

Inside the oak panelled reception area, the secretary asked me to take a seat while she called someone down. Within a few minutes, a large, round, bespectacled man wearing a three piece suit entered into the room smiling, and introduced himself as Mr Tidy, the personnel manager. He asked me one or two questions about myself; how old was I, where did I live and what sort of job would I like? Well I didn't want a job sitting at a bench all day, that's for sure, so I told him of my previous experience as a store man at The Rolex Paper Company. Wonderful! He said. 'We have a vacancy in the pharmaceuticals department for an assistant store man', and if I was interested he would take me over there for a look around. I was very interested, so off we went.

Well let me tell you! The inside of the factory is as interesting as the outside, and over the coming months, I spent many hours whilst doing my duties and errands exploring the, five floor plus basement, maze-like labyrinth of interconnecting corridors, passageways, staircases and lift shafts.

When we arrived at the pharmaceuticals store, Mr Tidy introduced me to the foreman Cyril Slater. I had to work out a weeks' notice at the garage, after which I commenced employment at Horlicks.

Richard Thomas who was the same age as me, worked in the stores and showed me the ropes for the first few weeks, and then we worked together and became best friends. There was also another older man who worked in the stores, who joined after me, called Charlie Pallet. During the War he had been a wireless operator in Lancaster Bombers and could also do 'Morse Code'. He used to tell us lots of stories, particularly about 'Intelligence' training, and quiz us with questions designed to trip you up. It was all very exciting! He was also a good letter writer and lived in a house close to the factory, with his wife and two sons. He worked in Horlicks until his retirement, becoming the head store man in the 'carton' stores. I saw him recently; he still lives in the same house and still looks the same, even though he is over 90.

Horlicks was a huge place, with lots of people working there, often related to each other; my friend, Richard had two brothers and a sister that worked elsewhere in the factory. It was like being part of a big family; also there were many youngsters, so I had lots of friends.

The pharmaceuticals' building which was an extension of the original, connected by an internal bridge, also housed 'the Mint' mint sauce, the old Slough family firm of Elliman's Embrocation, which was bought up in 1961, Tabasco sauce, and Airwick. One of our jobs in the stores was to provide the tablet room with the ingredients of whatever particular batch they were being asked to prepare.

There were, sometimes, preparations that required items from the 'Poison room' which of course needed to be authorised by at least two people; the foreman and one other person. Or on occasion, special liquids were required from the 'Distillery'. Substances were weighed in kilos, packaged, stacked on pallets and moved around on hand-pulled pallet trucks.

During the course of the day we had to travel to all parts of the factory fetching and delivering one thing or another; everything, from bottles, jars, phials, cartons and dividers, to powders and liquids etc. etc. either by sack barrow or pallet truck. We would traverse the buildings across the many levels via the network of lift shafts, which were always busy and invariably incurred long delays. A collection from the Distillery, at the far end of the factory on the ground floor, for example, would not unusually take 2 hours, but our foreman was very good, and never quizzed or questioned us if we were delayed. He was a nice old bloke; well I don't think he was that old really, probably about 50. He was tall, wore a brown overall and would sit at his desk with his head down, quietly and methodically getting on with his work.

He would cycle to work and was always on time, not like us youngsters, who were regularly late, then he would laugh and say: 'what's the matter, didn't your alarm go off?' We'd groan, thinking he was being sarcastic, but then we would at that age, wouldn't we? Poor old Cyril. His only pleasure was to go to the Slough Dog Track on a Thursday night, and meet his friends to have a bet and a smoke. That was the only time that he smoked a cigarette.

There was a period that we were quiet for a while, so Cyril sent me and Richard down to the basement to clear out some old stock to make a bit of space. The area of the basement was the floor size of the factory above it. It was great! He just left us down there for two weeks with instructions, and told us to get on with it, I bet he had a nice peaceful time, with us out from under his feet.

There was stuff in that basement that went back to Edwardian times: bottles, jars, mixing jugs and cups. There was even an old travelling chest with two handles, the type you see on ships. Everything on the list had to be taken up and over, and down to the 'Bank' then dumped in the skip. The 'Bank' was exactly that; situated in 'Despatch'.

Horlicks had its own railway sidings with a separate track alongside the bank at the Despatch bay, where a line of goods-wagons were shunted into position, and loaded by a team of about a dozen or so, who worked continuously in shifts.

The firm was self sufficient too; it had all its own maintenance staff and workshops, electrician, engineers and painters, a sprinkler system and its own D.C. electrical supply. There was also a very nice canteen on the top floor, a sports field and social club, a sick bay and Matron.

The security was overseen by Mr Gurney, who was 6ft and balding with a moustache, probably an ex military man, who wore a tweed jacket, shirt and tie and was very well turned out. He was assisted by his son, and he was very serious about his job; mind you, he did have a lot of it.

It was a Friday afternoon when our foreman sent us down to the 'goods inward' to receive a consignment of raw opium, packed into 9 -

50 lb (25kg) drums. It was hugely expensive and required to be collected and secured as a matter of urgency.

Well they shouldn't have sent boys down to do a man's job, because there was a mix up as to who was to take responsibility for it, and because at 4.30pm we clocked off and went home, the result was that the goods stayed outside in the delivery bay all weekend until Monday morning.

Coo! Talk about a flap. I wonder if Gurney knew about it. I often think about that balls-up; there were no security fences or gates around that part of the factory, which led straight onto the car park, then into the road. Imagine what that amount of opium would be worth today if it got into the wrong hands!

In the gardens was a big house that accommodated some of the staff. It was built at the same time as the factory in1908, and was originally occupied by Oliver Horlick, who was, then, in charge of the works.

Beechams bought up Horlicks in 1969 and has since demolished the house, and turned the land into a car park, then over time removed the entire track and sent their goods by road.

Sometime later, they dispensed with the bottling plant, closed all the small in-house industries and laid off all the workers. The Horlicks powder is now filled into one ton bags, stored in the factory and then sent to be packaged elsewhere. What a shame!

In the late 1960's the council installed into all their houses, three single 13A sockets, an electric light in the passage and the toilet, a gas fire in the front room and an immersion heater in the tank, which was previously heated by a back-boiler in the fireplace. Coal and paraffin, as a means of heating was becoming unpopular, probably because of the discovery of North Sea Oil. We were notified by the Gas board that the conversion from Town Gas to North Sea gas was under way and that a gas fitter would call in a few days time to change our meter.

When the fitter arrived it was my old school friend and fellow biker, Jimmy Hearn. We showed him in and he set to work in the meter cupboard. I remember feeling envious of him because he had a trade, and that his dad had just bought him a brand new bike (BSA C15 250cc) from Sid Moram's, but we were all a bit confused when we saw it completely stripped down in his back garden! He told us that he wanted to know what made it work.

Controllable gas at your fingertips and hot water at the flick of a switch were the buzz words of the day, and Ted Moult was advertising, and telling us the benefits of double-glazing. Very few people had central heating, and it would be another 20 years before it became affordable or standard in new-builds. When they did take off we wondered how we ever managed without them! Once we began to make our homes warmer and more comfortable, it was discovered through research that all that heat, without sufficient loft insulation was going straight out through the roof. We were 'paying to heat the sky'!

*

It's true that motorbikes are dangerous because if you get a knock, there is nothing to protect you. You have to have eyes in the back of your head and be very alert. I was out with Eddie Humphries one Saturday morning, following approximately 6 car lengths behind him in Stoke Poges Lane, just approaching Horlicks Bridge. As he passed a car in the lay-by it did a u-turn right in front of me. There was no time to brake; I saw the car in front of me, and then I was flying through the air.

The Bucks Constabulary were there in minutes and the ambulance arrived shortly after, as the crowd watched on and saw that I was still conscious the mood lightened and they began to joke, especially as they noticed that I couldn't take my eyes off the pretty young Police woman who was kneeling and making a fuss of me. Strangely, I felt no pain? The Ambulance driver strapped me up and took me to hospital, not to Upton hospital in town but to the new Wexham Park district hospital that had just recently opened and I was to be one of their first casualties.

It was such a long way from town that I didn't know how anybody was going to visit me, because many people didn't have cars then, in fact the car park only had provision for about 6 or 8 vehicles. I remember thinking then, that remote District hospitals were a bad idea, because they were too far out, they were too big and that when they close the entire small town and cottage hospitals, all the patients will converge in one place; it will probably become impersonal and a logistical nightmare. Anyway, I was examined at the hospital and it was discovered that there were no broken bones and that I'd received no serious injuries. I was discharged after a few hours, but not before the motorcycle policeman, who had escorted the ambulance to the hospital, gave me a road safety talk. I asked him for a lift home but he said that it wasn't allowed. I sat there for a while after he had left, completely on my own, thinking how desolate this place was, and was convinced that it would fail, because no one would ever come here.

I can't remember how I got home, I probably walked (a good hour to my house), and I certainly never told my mum about the incident. Can you imagine the distress that would have caused her?

Centralising resources this way instead of having local hospitals, from a patient's point of view, is a bad idea. There is a place for specialist hospitals, which are in London and other places I know, because no hospital can do everything, as in my sister's case, which I will tell you about shortly.

Wexham Park had a bad reputation from the start with botched operations, removal of the wrong limbs, wrong patient; the place was too big; the left hand didn't know what the right hand was doing. It was a joke, like something out of a carry-on film, only nobody was laughing. It started to improve in the 1980's when they built a school for teaching the student nurses, recruited locally; then they began to recruit from Ireland. These days, Matron has disappeared as has the school, the wards are infected and the personnel comes from abroad. It's not only in nursing that we no longer train up our own, it is the same across the board. Without training or apprenticeships the politicians of the main parties have created an underclass by preferring to bring in foreign workers already trained, we therefore are losing the ability and knowledge to provide and look after ourselves. Not only is it wrong, it doesn't make sense.

*

All the bikes were lined up outside the youth club with 'L' plates on, as we stood and pondered the idea of taking our tests, after all, at aged between 17 and 19, with a year or two's experience we considered ourselves accomplished riders and were outgrowing our 250's anyway. We were waiting for Jimmy Hearn to show up because he had taken his test earlier in the day, and we were anxious to know how he got on. As he came up the drive we could see the bright red L plates still on, he looked quite miserable as he pulled up, and just shook his head. We gave him a minute or two to park up and take his helmet off, and then we began to ask him about the test.

He'd chosen to take the test in Slough as he was familiar with the route. He had to demonstrate good road sense, signalling and positioning, appear confident and be in control of his machine at all times. This was tested by his ability to perform an effective 'emergency stop'. The examiner gave him a route and said: 'I will step out into the road in front of you and hold up my clipboard; you won't know when or where I will appear but, the minute you see me, you must immediately brake and bring your machine to a controlled stop'. Well! What happened? We asked; did you knock him down? No, he said. 'I passed!' then removed his L plates.

This encouraged us to apply, which I did straight away; receiving my test date for six weeks time, which I also passed. Now for a new bike! My preference, when it came to bigger bikes, was the Triumph. I went to Sid Moram's to see what they had in stock, and came away with a large colour poster, showing the latest three models, which I put up in my bedroom. The three bikes on the poster were: the Tiger 100, 500cc – Daytona, 500cc – and Bonneville 650cc. With the caption '1968 Triumphs are for men only; see how they run'. I dreamt of one day being able to afford one, but it was just a dream. A new Triumph T100 was £300; there was no way I could afford that on £10 a week, still, I carried on dreaming.

There was always a chance of winning on Premium Bonds; one of my £5's worth would surely get drawn one day.

Around August the following year, Trevor Isaacs turned up at the club, one night, on a Honda 90cc with a box on the back, which he used for carrying newspapers. It was brand new, and went like a rocket. All he had to do was take newspapers to the dispensers around town, for which he earned more money than me, had the use of the bike and didn't have to fork out for petrol, and there was a vacancy. It sounded perfect; the bike was a bit small, but with the extra money, I'd be able to save about a Fiver a week and in just over a year I'd have enough money to buy a Triumph Tiger.

The next day I called into the office of the *Evening Mail* and was interviewed by the Editor for the job, he showed a particular interest in me because I was wearing my motorcycling gear. I told him that I rode a bike, and that my friend had told me of the vacancy. Unfortunately, he said, that job was no longer available. There was however, a vacancy for a despatch rider, which involved running news items and deadlines to the printers, and asked had I passed my test, because the bikes used for that job were 'speed twins'. He was an old biker, and the term that he had just used 'speed twin' was for what was now the T100. I sat up astonished, with my mouth open! stuttering out: 'no, no I couldn't! I haven't ridden anything that powerful before'. It was a bit of a shock and all a bit too soon. He said: 'you've passed your test haven't you? If you want the job it's yours. Come here tomorrow morning and I'll arrange a test ride for you'.

The next day I arrived at 9 a.m. to meet the other rider that was to take me out, and was surprised to see that it was Jimmy Ellis, an older boy who used to go to William Penn. Well I knew him because he only lived around the corner from me. He was a Biker, and so was his dad before him who knew my family well, especially what a rotter my Dad was. It's a small world isn't it? There were two T100's; Jim rode one of them, and mine, the other one, was at 'Sid's' being serviced so we went together to collect it. It was beautiful! Aqua-marine and gleaming! just 'run-in', with barely 1,000 miles on the clock; Jim 'kicked it over' and it breathed into life with a rapid 'thump, thump, thump, thump' which was like music to my ears. It was bigger than the 'Arrow', responsive and more powerful.

Jim could see that I was a little apprehensive but urged me on. 'Come on' he said, 'just follow me and go slowly for a while, you'll soon get used to it'. By the time I got to the end of the road I felt completely comfortable with it; it accelerated, it braked and it sailed around corners. I loved it; it was a pure thoroughbred. In 1969, and having passsed your test you were no longer restricted to riding anything up to 250cc, the L plates could be removed and you were now allowed to carry a pillion. Well I had no end of female passengers from then on; to the envy of my mates I'm sure, and occasionally I'd carry someone on the back if their bike had broken down.

Anyway, it was one Saturday when Mick Carpenter had his engine stripped down, that we were out on the bike in the pouring rain. It was the week of the first ever Music festival in Windsor Great Park, so we thought we'd have a ride out to take a look. When we got there, all we saw in the undulating fields were hundreds of tents, and people milling about ankle deep in mud soaking wet. We could hear the music in the distance and began walking towards it, but after five or ten minutes we still couldn't see the stage, just more tents and 'spaced out' Beatniks, or were they called Hippies then? I'm not sure when the change over occurred; 'Peace and Love man' Far out.

It was late in the afternoon by now and Mick wanted to see his girlfriend, she was at Susan Jones' house, so we saddled up and made tracks. The problem was, he was over two hours late, and we needed an excuse. 'I know' he said 'let's say that the heavy rain got into the exhaust pipes and we broke down'. 'Is that possible?' I replied. He was sure that that excuse would work, but just in case I sat outside whilst he went in. Mick rode around with me for a while until his bike was back on the road; one of our favourite haunts was The Jack cafe in King Street, (near Nicholson Walk) Maidenhead; it had a couple of pin tables and a great Jukebox. It's not there anymore, but it was a popular Bikers meeting place, although by now, the Rockers had been replaced by the more 'rough and rugged' Hells Angels which made the place feel more like a saloon bar in the Wild West, where the saddle tramps had traded their horses for Harley Davidson's.

It was the following Thursday night that I took Mick to see his girlfriend again at Susan's house. I was only 17 and not as adept with the girls as he, and at that age my passion was motorbikes, and my interests were the Youth club and my mates. I was quite happy sitting outside on my bike, minding my own business, but Susan had other ideas and came bouncing down the path to talk to me because I 'looked lonely'. 'Come inside' she said. 'We're about to watch Top of the Pops' she pronounced. 'Bring your bike into the garden' she urged. I wasn't lonely, I didn't want to watch telly and I didn't want to heave my bike up the kerb and into the garden. Then Mick and Marion came to the front door and joined in the plea; I was trounced! She was cheerful, spoke awfully posh and I did fancy her, so I gave way in the face of overwhelming desire! I mean force.

When it was time to leave, we had a kiss and a cuddle in the kitchen by the back door, and then it was obvious to us both that we were attracted to each other. She was my first girlfriend, I was serious about her and thought that we would eventually marry, but it wasn't to be. Our encounter was only to last six months, because after all we were very young. I was pretty cut up about us splitting up, but over time I accepted it as one of life's many experiences and got on with my life, until her uncle Reg, who I still see regularly, told me that she had recently died. I was surprised at how deeply affected I was. I am so glad that she was in my life, because even in that short time, she had a profound impact on me that was to affect the rest of my life.

When I first met Susan, she had only recently lost her Dad (Frank) three years earlier and talked of him frequently. Her brother Robert at the age of only 14 dutifully assumed the role of 'Man of the House', which was unhappily thrust upon him by his Father's untimely passing. I felt that the family were having a tough time of it; their father's premature death had left their mother and young family of four stranded, the youngest being only three years old at the time. They were a very close family and he was sorely missed, by none more than by his younger brother Reg, whose life fell apart after losing his only brother at such a young age. It's very sad. When I first met Susan's uncle Reg at her house, he told me that he knew my Dad and that they had worked together digging out the Cells at the new Slough Police Station in the 1950's and that when completed, my Dad was one of the first occupants. That's not something you want too many people to know about is it?

Frank was only 41 when he died in 1966, and his early death was attributed to the treatment that he received whilst in captivity during the war. In 1939, at his home in Liverpool Frank, at the age of 14, joined the Royal Navy's Boys Unit and trained at the Cunningham Camp in the Isle of Man.

At 17 Frank was serving on *HMS Prince of Wales*, when it was dispatched to Singapore, on the 25th October 1941, to deter the Japanese from attacking Malaya and the East Indies, becoming the Flagship of the Eastern Fleet under Admiral Sir Tom Philips.

Force Z, as they were called, tried unsuccessfully, to intercept the Japanese landing fleets, and on the 10th December 1941 whilst returning to Singapore, were attacked and sunk by 86 Japanese bombers. The Destroyer, *HMS Express* moved in to pick up survivors; 327 were lost, including Admiral Tom Philips and Captain John Leach, who chose to go down with their ship. It was to be the greatest British Naval disaster of the 2nd World War.

Singapore fell to the Japanese, two months later, on the 15th February 1942 and Frank was taken and held as a POW for three and a half years until the end of the war. While a prisoner, he contracted malaria, dysentery, and other tropical diseases that contributed to the shortening of his life.

Although Reg was 5 years younger than Frank and didn't serve in the 2nd world war, he did later see action in the Korean War as a member of a tank crew. Frank had told Reg that he bore no malice, nor held any resentment towards the Japanese as they were treated as harshly and ate the same food rations. Being a kind and compassionate human being he probably failed to notice that his captors weren't required to work until they dropped.

*

As 1969 drew to close and the weather got bad the newspaper (*Evening Mail*) company switched from bikes to Mini vans, which were also useful for delivering bundles of newspapers. They also changed printers which consequently changed the nature of the job.

I decided that I'd had the best of the job, which had been great during the summer months, but it was time to move on. I tried several other jobs over the next few months, but couldn't find anything suitable.

There was a job at Weekes' Farm, who had their own slaughter house, as a trainee Butcher; a trainee managers job at Lenard's shoe shop and several others, and that's how it went for a while. Meanwhile, Susan went off to work away as a Nanny and broke my heart.

My sister's illness

One night in the spring of last year (1969), my sister Jill came home from work unusually tired, but never one to complain, took a couple of aspirin and went to bed early. The next day she felt a little better and set off to work, but she took ill again and was sent home after a few hours. My mum decided to call in the Doctor who concluded that it might be 'Asian flu' but referred her to Wexham Park for tests.

Three days later she was transferred to a specialist ward in Fulham Hospital for further tests. Back then the Patient and their family weren't informed of the findings, probably because their findings were based on pure speculation, and in my sister's case it was a matter of a series of experiments using the latest drugs. At one point she was kept in isolation in a sterile unit, room 4, where we could only talk to her through the 1ft sq window of the door.

This went on for months until one day my mum begged the Ward Sister for more information that she, incidentally, wasn't allowed to give, but eventually, an appointment was made for her to see the Doctor. The doctor explained that the blood count was too high; there were too many white cells and that all they could do was to keep trying different drugs until they got a positive reaction. He assured my mum that new drugs were being discovered every day, and in fact, they were expecting some from America very soon.

My sister asked to be moved to the 'ward' despite being warned that it could hamper her recovery, but by this time she had reconciled herself to the fact that, if she was to be a long term patient, she would like to be among other girls of her age. On the ward, the patients in the first five beds either side were young girls with the same symptoms, receiving similar treatment but none were being cured; they were dying one after the other.

Very soon my sister's condition began to worsen. They had detected cancerous cells in the womb, and declared that immediate surgery was necessary to save her life. We were all devastated, although my mum's immediate concern was that my sister would never have children, but at least the Doctor had said something positive and given us a glimmer of hope. It was possible, that now they had found something tangible, my sister's chances of survival would increase, but the uncomfortable truth was that they didn't know how to treat this 'illness'. Like in the early days of medicine, it was a case of trial and error.

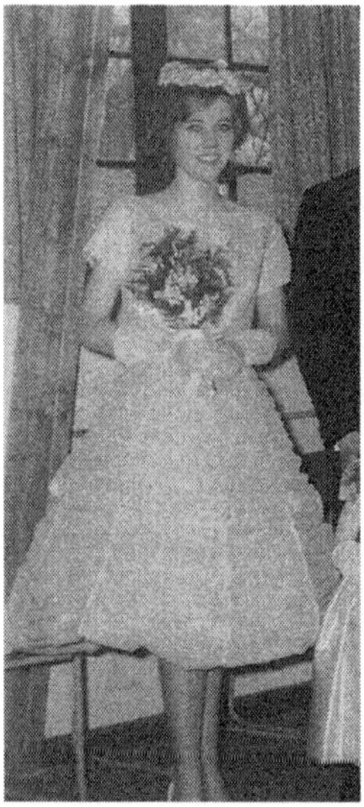

Jill as a bridesmaid at our sister June's wedding

They kept my poor sister alive for 17 months, even though most of the time she was in a lot of pain. She finally succumbed to her illness, and passed away on 15th August 1970, aged 24.

My mum had lost several babies at birth and two infants; it wasn't uncommon in those days, as infant mortality rates were quite high, but she never got over losing Jill. A few weeks before my sister died, and when her condition began to deteriorate, we all, together with my mum decided that the 'Old Man' should be told. Now remember, he hadn't had any part in our upbringing, but mother said: 'we were in love once;

he's the father of all my children, and it's only right that he should have the right to see Lillian, as he would call her, while there's still time'. First we had to find him!

He hadn't lived in Slough for years; he could be anywhere. I don't know how, but we eventually tracked him down, and found him.

John Henry (Jackie) Wight, Number 042584

He was being detained at Her Majesty's pleasure, at HM Prison Wandsworth, London SW18. My Brother in-Law, Mick, took the day off work to take us all in his car, on the way to the hospital, to pick my dad up outside the prison gates, who was standing there handcuffed to a prison warden (how degrading) under strict instructions that he return at the stated time. Soon after on the 8th August my mum received a letter from my dad in 'Wandsworth', he wrote:

Dear Rose,
Just a line to let you know I arrived back safe and sound. But sorry I kept you waiting for a letter, still better late than never. I was so pleased to see Lillian, and do hope she gets over this, as I won't be settled till she is. There is one good thing, I have not long to do so will be able to see her every day.
I hope you got back home OK, and you want to take it easy otherwise you will make yourself ill, and that won't do. Everybody was asking me how Lil was and one of the boys told the priest how ill she was, and a special prayer was said, so that was nice wasn't it? Well dear, let's hope she will pull through, I am always thinking about you and the family.
So Jackie has had a baby? Well that was news to me! She looked well when I seen her, and our June just looked lovely. I am so pleased she is getting on well, as she deserves it, but I must say, Mick is a nice chap and I know he will look after June. Tell June and Mick I was asking after them.

As regards Rita, well I don't know what to think, but I am still worried about her, I only wish she would try and be sensible, she is so young and looks like spoiling her life. It does not matter now what I have done, I have paid for it. But I don't like to see my children in any sort of trouble, so tell her what I have said.
I will be down to see you just as soon as I have finished my term, which should be Nov 26th then we will see what can be done. You must keep in touch with me so that I will know how things are. You can always drop me a line and I will do my best to answer.
I arrived back here at ten to five, so everything was OK. Tell Jim and Ken I was asking after them, and to stick to their jobs and be good, which I know they are. Remember what I said to you at the hospital, well that still stands, but I can't do anything till we are together again. If you are of the same mind, things should work out alright. We have got to think of the family. Poor Jim needs a father, remember, he is the baby of the family, the others are old enough to look after themselves.
Well Rose, things are much the same, and I am looking forward to seeing you all again. So if you get time drop me a line, I will always answer back.
Well dear, I can't think of much more to say. Try not to worry and hope that everything will turn out for the best. Remember me to all at home. Don't forget to tell Rita what I said, so cheerio for now. Love to Lil and all.
I remain as always
Jackie xx
xxxxxx
xxxxx
xxxx
xx

It was over 10 years since the divorce. What was in his mind; what sort of man was this? It's clear from this letter (which has only recently come to light, during the course of my research and retrieval for this book) that he still loved his wife and family. Had he finally seen the error of his ways?

I didn't see him again for another couple of years until he turned up in Slough and took a job in 'Coopers Mechanical Joints' on the Trading Estate where he worked for a further 2 or 3 years before he himself became ill and died. During that time he came to the house to plead with my mum to take him back, but she wouldn't go to the door, instead me and Jim had to ask him to leave.

When we were told that he was terminally ill in Wexham Park Hospital all the family paid him a visit. He lost weight and went downhill rapidly, and when on his deathbed my mum sat by his side holding his hand he said: 'well Rose, we're still here together; let's make another go of it; let's get remarried, what do you say?' My mum agreed and said 'yes, ok'.

Afterwards she told us, that because he was dying, she didn't want to upset him? Sitting next to her years later, in fact, not long before she herself died, she told me that she wished she had made up with the 'old man'. Well I was shocked to hear her say that, and in return said: 'how can you say that after the rotten life he gave you?' to which she replied: 'you were only young! You don't understand! We had our good times. 'But' I said 'knowing what you know now, would you have done things differently; had all those kids?' Her answer? 'We were in love and the children were my life'. Well, what do I know? I just let it rest there.

The way our dad treated us made me feel not worthy, lowly and not worth bothering about. There were much better families than ours weren't there? Proper families! We knew this, by the way that some people looked at, and treated, us. Some would let us know verbally what they thought of a family with no man about the house.

The stigma of having an absent father, of being in prison or having an illegitimate child were so great in those days, that it was easier to bow down, know your place and keep quiet; or maybe tell a few white lies to ease the shame, and many did. You would say for example: that an absent father was 'away at sea' or that an illegitimate child was your brother or sister.

There was no provision for underage pregnancies, or unmarried mothers, these things were always kept quiet, very often with both mother and child being cared for by her parents in the family home. The alternative was, for the child to be taken into care, and for the mother to be placed in an institution.

Adulthood

By the age of 18, the girl that I wanted to marry had dumped me; not good enough was I? My sister had died at 24 years old, and my dad had gone off with another woman because he thought she had money. How much worse could it get? Did our family have the mark of Cain on it?

After these cruel series of events however, my life began to change dramatically for the better. I became more proficient at my job and had money in my pocket; I had bettered myself! Along with the confidence though, came resentment, then I started to get angry and rebellious, because I wasn't a kid anymore was I? Now, as an adult these people didn't look so high and mighty; now, I could stand up to the bullies and fight back, and I did. Almost every week I'd punch someone out if they tried to put me down (I wonder where I got that from?).

Shoplifting came next even though I had enough money to pay! I wanted to rub their noses in it for the life they'd given my mum. This period continued for about 18 months; I got in trouble with the police and they'd hound me. It got to the point where I couldn't leave the house without getting pulled up and questioned. I was becoming like my dad, it had to stop! I wasn't like him.

I wasn't proud of that brief bad episode in my life and strongly believe it was because of the lack of guidance from a father figure. But I put it behind me and strived on with confidence. My dad had a lot to answer for I thought, but had he inadvertently made me what I am? Who knows? This much I did know; I was an adult now and had to be responsible for my actions because they had consequences. There was no one else to blame anymore.

The 1970 general election was held on the 18th June, and was to be the first in which 18 year olds were allowed to vote, me being one of them, because up until the 'Representation of the Peoples Act 1969' only 21year olds or over were permitted to vote. The Labour party, ahead in the polls, were tipped to win. So, probably, because of the hugely unpopular introduction of decimalisation, which his government had been responsible for, due in 1971, Wilson called for an early election to maximise his vote.

This surprised the Conservatives, who were expecting an October election. But they needn't have worried, because the extensive coverage and attention paid to Enoch Powell, is estimated to have attracted an extra 2.5 million votes.

Whilst I continued my search for a suitable job, I ran into an old friend from Horlicks. His name was Carl and he was the foreman of the 'carton' stores before Charlie Pallet took over the job later on. It was the usual chatter, you know, how are you? Long time no see etc. It had been less than a year since I'd seen him, but it felt longer, so we had a good chat, and during our 'catching-up' session he offered me a job; so it was back to Horlicks. When I got back there it felt good because I knew lots of people, even my brother Jimmy was working there. I started pretty much straight away on £13 a week. The great thing about working in a large factory, I mean there in particular, was the camaraderie and the security; it was a job for life if you wanted it to be.

A lot of people who lived in Slough then, probably worked there too, because almost everyone either walked or cycled to work. You would bump into people in work that you knew, or who knew your family, so I wasn't too surprised when I bumped into Jimmy Hearn's mum in one of the departments. She told me how well he was doing at the Gas Board; that he goes out on jobs on his own now, and would be taking his exams at college soon to become a qualified Gas Fitter. That's when I told her that I'd always wanted to be an Electrician but was unable to get an apprenticeship, but she encouraged me by saying that it's never too late; you could always go as an 'Electricians mate' and learn your trade that way. What a lovely woman, to have given me that idea! Anyway, that was something to think about, but for now I had to sort out my social life. The Orchard was a good place to start. I fitted right back in, although, it did feel different. I'd changed, grown up a little bit and I missed my life with Susan awfully. I was always wondering where she was or what she was doing? But life moves on doesn't it? I was catching up with old, and meeting new friends at a rapid pace, not that I was trying too hard, I just sort of went along with the flow of things.

My life was changing at an interesting and exciting pace, it was amazing! The Carlton Ballroom in Slough had been closed down for a while, but the news quickly got around that it had recently reopened as a Disco, with a 10 shilling (50p) entrance fee, so that's where we all went off to on a Friday night. Reggae was popular then and that's what was played; all the black boys would be in the side aisle smoking their 'joints' and getting stoned, and all the white boys would be at the bar getting drunk, while me and my mates would be on the dance floor with the girls.

The Orchard closed down for a few months for renovations so we transferred to the Upton Lea youth club while the work was being carried out. Although it was off our patch, we blended in okay because we knew quite a few of the kids from the Carlton, or from work, plus we made new friends; and girlfriends. Eric Collins and Peter Smith were friends that I met up with, who I hadn't seen since school. I think we all used to meet up in the 'Good Companions' pub (Goodies) and go on from there.

Manor Park, the area that I grew up in, had a reputation for being tough but I didn't find it that bad, because we all either knew or recognised each other. A bit like the 'Wild West' really, you'd soon spot an unfamiliar face in town. I liked Eric Collins and got on with him well, he was a great character, dependable and reliable, and would never back down from a fight. In the club one night one of the Upton Lea boys (Roydon) who was one of our friends anyway, and a bit of a Boxer, took a dislike to Eric, for some reason or another, and wanted to fight him outside. I was asked to pass the message on; although Roydon was much bigger, Eric wasn't in the least bit bothered. He just casually took up the challenge without a word and got stuck in.

Afterwards, he came back in and carried on as if nothing had happened. You won't ever stop people fighting, but what was better then was that it was just a fist fight; no knives, tools or guns; no cyber-bullying or threatening phone calls, it just kicked off and you made up, or went your separate ways. Peter Smith and I became good friends and went out a lot together chatting up the girls. Peter lived in my Street and went to the same school, but we'd only started hanging around together in the last few months.

We were good mates and soon began going out with two girls, Pat and Francis, who were sisters. I went out with Pat Doyle for almost a year, she was a great girl. She was popular and well liked, and unbeknown to me, our families knew each other, and thought that we would marry; and we should have, and probably would have if I had met her before Susan.

My sisters said that I had met her on the rebound, but I didn't feel that was true, because I was a completely different person from before and a lot harder, but in spite of that, we were in love and had a great relationship, but it was never going to ever be the same was it? Poor Pat.

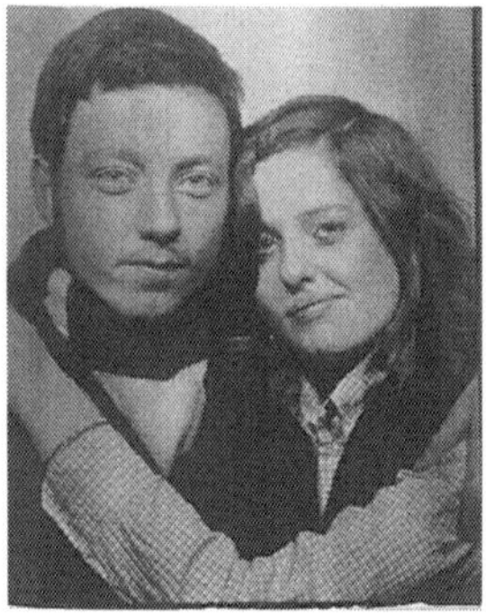

Me and Pat

I'd like to know what happened to Ginger Harman. He was one of the five of us that went to Hayling Island in Deverill's Minivan; a trip we made regularly, slept overnight in the vehicles and drove back the next day. On the way back from one of these trips, we came upon an unusually long tailback of traffic on the A30 near Bagshot; we thought then that it must have been a massive pile-up, and because our turn-off was at Egham and through Windsor, it wasn't until much later that we discovered that the Trident airliner, *Papa India*, crashed near Staines just after 4pm on the 18th June 1972, a few minutes after taking off from Heathrow airport, killing all on board.

*

A group of us met in the Farnham Road one evening and got onto the bus into Slough and, together, began talking about what we had achieved since leaving school. Keith West was an apprentice Plumber; Alan Deverill was a trainee mechanic and remained at that same garage until two years ago, when he was made redundant, because the boss retired and closed down the business, selling the land to property developers. When it came to my turn, I told them of the different jobs I'd had and that what I really wanted, was to be an electrician. (I had known as a fourteen year old that I wanted to be an Electrician, because whilst trying to connect a pendant in my bedroom, after turning off the electric light switch, I got an electric shock that made me fall off the chair. I was puzzled, and wanted to know and understand why that had happened.) Having had no luck so far, I thought that I had probably missed the boat by now, but then Alan came back with the following: 'my dad's friend is an electrician; he's starting a new contract shortly and is looking for a mate'. I was definitely interested, so Alan's dad contacted his friend Lou Ashton to arrange for a meeting for the following week.

Keith borrowed his dad's car and we all went to Lou's house, where we spent the evening chatting and drinking tea.

Lou with his wife Audrey and young family

Lou asked me lots of questions and when he was satisfied that I would be suitable, offered me the job for £15 a week, which was £2 a week more than I was getting from Horlicks. I owe a debt of gratitude to Lou that I can never hope to repay. He took me on and trained me up at a time when no one else was interested. Unbelievable! What luck! I started in September 1970. Once settled into the job, I then enrolled at Slough College of Technology on day-release.

Lou died on the 30th December 2010, bereft, sad and lonely after losing his wife a few years earlier. I'd visit him reguarly and would frequently remind him of how grateful I was to him for having confidence in me and giving me a chance. It was a life changing experience, and probably one of the best days of my life.

*

Sid Morton was my best mate at college and at break times we'd go to the ABC tea rooms or Tony's Grill for lunch that, I swear, made the best coffee in town. Sid was the happiest bloke I know. He was always telling jokes, impersonating Elvis or singing Benny Hill's 'Ernie' (the fastest milkman in the west). These days he calls himself the 'Musicman' and plays his guitar in pubs around the town.

I loved my job and had definitely made the right career choice. Even before my final exams, I was in charge of jobs at work, and re-wiring houses on the weekend; starting on a Friday night and finishing on a Sunday night, and I was getting well paid for doing something that I really enjoyed. Once the word got round, I was in constant demand, because I was probably working well below the going rate, so everyone was happy. Also, I was providing a valuable service at a reasonable price whilst gaining invaluable experience.

Susan Jones dumping me like that changed my life, and I don't think for the better. I had many more girlfriends afterwards, but never totally committed myself to any one of them. When I finished with Pat to go out with Gina, she told me that I would go through my life breaking girl's hearts, and end up a lonely old man. Well she was partly right, because I am on my own now and feel lonely at times, but I do have my son, who I look after as a single parent. Mine and Gina's relationship in the summer of 1971 was destined to be short lived, because her parents sold up and the family went back to Italy. The weather that summer was glorious so we spent a lot of time on the bike. Even on the bike it was shirtsleeve weather and no need to wear crash helmets because it wasn't compulsory to do so then.

Gina

We rode everywhere together, stopping off at cafes along the way for a cup of tea and snacks (Gina always drank coffee); Burnham Beeches, West Wycombe and that café in Uxbridge station, which I mentioned earlier, were among our favourite places to visit.

A moment that I remember vividly was, travelling along the A40 on the way to Uxbridge, cruising down the hill at Bakers wood towards Denham with the sun high in the cloudless blue sky and a warm breeze in our hair; Gina's arms wrapped firmly around my waist with her head resting on my shoulder that time seemed to freeze. I felt we were sailing, this was pure heaven.

After Gina went back to Italy in September 1971 I found myself, once again, free and single; and young; I was only 20, so got stuck into my work, riding my bike and meeting my friends down at the youth club, tagging as many young fillies as was possible.

At that age I could never envisage becoming old because I was totally and utterly absorbed with living in the moment; absolute and pure magic! The brutal reality was that time marches on, and that on my next birthday I would be 21 and would have to leave the youth club.

Mick Carpenter, who was a couple of years older than me had since left the 'Orchard' and married his girlfriend Anita, and I supposed we all thought that we would do the same, after all, that was the age of adulthood then, and the time to settle down.

Realising this, when I was assigned to my next job at 'Vitramon' in Wooburn Green, Bucks., near High Wycombe I had the overwhelming feeling that I was about to meet my future wife. Well, when I arrived there I found that the factory was full of girls, so was pretty much spoilt for choice.

The girl that I fell for, in the end, was Mary O'Driscoll with whom I went steady with for two and a half years, but unfortunately I couldn't see myself tying the knot and remaining together for the long haul, so went out with her mate Christine, but that ended after about 12 months. By now I was becoming tired of being in dead end relationships and decided not to go out with any girls for a while, but hang out with the boys instead.

It was around this time that I met up with some new friends on my estate, and became best friends with Dave Skinner. One of our favourite places to go was the 'Snooker Spot'. It had about a dozen tables and a snack bar, adjacent to which were the club rules chalked up on a board; it read: No Loud talking – No Alcohol – No Girls - No Swearing – No Spitting – No Music and no Fighting etc.

Well, all was fine in the Snooker Spot 99.9% of the time until, inevitably, you got some show-offs or trouble-makers trying to throw their weight around. Now Dave was a great bloke; 6ft 4 inches, strongly built with a very kind nature; a gentle giant. He didn't rile easily, was certainly not aggressive, and I never saw him lose his temper. But one night while playing snooker, he was picked on by some twit who had goaded him night after night for about a week; Dave remained passive, which only gave this bullyboy more confidence, until he laid his hands on Dave who then swung with a left hook, sending the twit bowling across the floor. And that was the end of that.

Over the years, I bump into Dave and we have a good chat and catch up. Not having seen him for while, I made some enquiries around town as to his whereabouts and was quite shocked to hear that he was in hospital and had just undergone a major operation. I visited him the next day to find him in a lot of pain but in good spirits.

*

For a spell I worked at Schwarzkopf in Aylesbury for the High Wycombe branch of Manpower, where I met and became friends with Chris Ponter, an 'electro/mechanical fitter'. Any time that we worked together, he would kick his legs high above his head, and do these lightning-fast punches straight from the hip, that looked like pistons firing out. He explained to me, that this was a style of Karate called Wadoryu. Apart from the James Bond films, Karate was pretty much unheard of.

Each Tuesday and Thursday after work, he'd get on the train to London to go training. He kept asking me to go with him, then after a while I decided to give it a try. The club was in Forest Gate in the East End of London; it was a bit of a trek, but once I'd met Peter Spanton, the 3rd level Dan black-belt instructor and joined in one of the lessons, I was hooked. It was highly desciplined and gave me somewhere to channel my energy. I stayed there for two and a half years, reaching brown belt level, before deciding to find somewhere closer to home. I was reluctant to change styles, but on finding the Slough Shotokan Club and watching them train with such power and precision, I joined up and still train today.

The Karate Union of Great Britain (KUGB) is the largest and most successful single-style association in the country with currently around 7,000 male and female members of all ages. My son, who is also a black belt, trains regularly and is on the English squad.

*

During the Conservative Government of 1970-74, particularly in 72 and 73, the British economy was troubled by high rates of inflation. Furthermore, the government led by Edward Heath failed to cut back on welfare spending. At one point the squeeze in the education budget resulted in Margaret Thatcher, then Secretary of State for Education, taking away free school milk from 8 to 11 year olds after which she was referred to as "Margaret Thatcher the Milk Snatcher".

By the middle of 1973, the National Union of Mineworkers had encouraged their members to work to rule, as a result coal stocks slowly dwindled, against a background of a quadrupling of Arab oil prices, strikes broke out everywhere.

To reduce electricity consumption, and thus conserve coal stocks, a series of measures were announced on the 13th December 1973. Heath's government instituted the three-day-week with the intent of prolonging the life of available fuel stocks. This reduction of the working week never affected me at all, because by this time I was employed in Agency work with Manpower and managed to work throughout.

With the country on reduced hours, and rubbish piling up in the streets, the miners flexed their muscles and threatened to bring the Heath government down. Throughout this period we were all encouraged to conserve energy in the home. Little stickers were placed on light switches telling us to switch off when leaving the room and stickers on telephones telling us not to use the phone during peak hours between 9am and 6pm; not that many people had their own phones in any case. Television companies were told to stop broadcasting after 10.30pm, so the telly went off and most had an early night, which created a bit of a baby boom.

I don't think most of these measures caused too much upset or disruption though. The real problems started when petrol rationing was introduced, causing panic buying, and massive queues during the restricted opening hours which led to frustration and punch-ups on the forecourt.

The national speed limit was reduced to improve petrol consumption, which at that time was only 35p a gallon (7p/litre) but rising rapidly, and as a consequence, all the big saloon cars began to disappear off the roads in favour of the more compact hatchbacks which were rising in popularity; at that time you could buy a big second hand Jaguar for a pittance, and those that couldn't be sold or given away were often seen in gardens or drives just rotting away.

Almost as soon as being elected, Heath applied to join the European Economic Community (common market) and was successful in signing the first of the 6 Treaties 'the European Communities Act 1972' culminating in the 6th and final 'Lisbon Treaty' which was really the renamed EU constitution, taking us fully into political union with the EU.

Edward Heath had the nerve to promise that "no loss of essential sovereignty" was involved in the passing of the 1972 act. Harold Wilson said the same thing during the 1975 Referendum campaign. Both Prime Ministers pretended we had merely joined a Common Market.

I fear Margaret Thatcher was deceived as to the way the Single European Act of 1986 would be used, which created the system of Qualified Majority Voting.

John Major then misled us about the Maastricht Treaty of 1992, and Tony Blair misled us over the Amsterdam Treaty of 1997 and the Nice Treaty of 2002.

It has always been essential to keep the true nature of the Project from the British people. They have to be slowly sucked into the embrace of the corrupt octupus, until it is too late to escape. That is the very essence of the project and I trust you will agree it is working very well.

Jean Monnet founding father of the EU said: "Europe's nations should be guided towards the superstate without their people understanding what is happening. This can be accomplished by successive steps, each disguised as having an economic purpose, but which will eventually and irreversibly lead to federation".

The following quotations show that Mr Heath was extremely deceitful with the people when describing the European project to them.

1970 "there will be no blueprint for a federal Europe".

1971 "there is no question of any erosion of essential sovereignty".

"There are some in this country who fear that, in going into Europe, we shall in some way sacrifice independence and sovereignty. These fears, I need hardly say, are completely unjustified".

1975 "there is no danger of a single currency"

In an interview with Peter Sissons, 1st November 1991:
Sissons, "the single currency, the United States of Europe: was that on your mind when you took Britain in?"
Heath, "Of course, yes."

All subsequent Prime Ministers have continued in this tradition.

The essence of Britain's relationship with the EU is contained in the European Communities Act of 1972 which outsources much of our lawmaking to the EU institutions and states these and all future EU laws become binding on Britain in their entirety "without further enactment". Whilst that clause remains in force, Parliament has little or no say in those laws which the EU chooses to impose on us.

City & Guilds

Passing my City & Guilds exam and receiving my Electrical craftsman certificate, was probably one of my finest achievements.

Mr Walker, the head of the Electrical Engineering department handed me my certificate saying: "here you are Mr Wight, you've done it, you are now a fully qualified electrician". It was the most amazing feeling of accomplishment, considering my background, and initial struggles to eventually find someone who was prepared to give me a chance. I'd made it by sticking to it and working hard at a job I thoroughly enjoyed, that also paid well. Thanks Lou.

Mr Walker added: "you can be proud of yourself; with this certificate you can go anywhere, it is an internationally recognised qualification, even in America". Well, that was a very liberating endorsement, I can tell you. I felt honoured. I didn't feel like travelling, but I wanted to leave site-work to broaden my horizons, and was keen to gain experience in industrial and commercial installations, and the opportunity to do that was right here on my doorstep; the Slough Trading Estate.

By far the best way to gain the maximum and most varied amount of experience I found, was to join the 'Manpower' employment agency who employed me directly, and whom I stayed with for 2-3years; sending me out, on mostly short term contracts. I was in heaven; working in big companies like: the Mars factory, Capseals, Westerns Biscuit Factory (makers of 'wagon wheels, and jammy dodgers, etc), the

Ladybird factory, Citroen, Fords, Dunlopillow, Aspros and many, many more.

If at any time they couldn't find me a placement immediately at the end of a particular contract, instead of being idle, I'd volunteer to do any job (given a choice, obviously) on their books, whether it was warehouse work, deliveries or forklift driving, and was still paid electrician's wages; talk about variety! It was bloody marvellous! This was a time when we had a massive industry, and actually made things that were stamped up "Made in England" where did we go wrong?

*

One evening during the autumn 1975 there were a few of us sitting around in Keith's house discussing our summer holidays. Keith was telling us about the summer holiday he'd had with his family in Scotland. That one afternoon after a day out, and as he and his cousin were old enough, they were allowed to stay out a little longer to fish at Loch Ness, while the rest of the family went back to their cottage for tea.

Having previously read all the reports about the Loch Ness Monster, they were hoping to catch a glimpse of 'Nessy' in the early evening when things quietened down a bit, but as the evening wore on, and they had still had no sighting, they began to wonder why their parents hadn't arrived to pick them up.

It was now dusk and they had to make a decision as to whether to wait, or take a short-cut along the hill path and get back before dark. Don't forget, there were no means of communication. They decided to set off on foot, and as they trekked the hill path that climbed away from the Loch, they looked back to see how far and how high they had risen, when with horror, they had full view of the road below and the solitary vehicle heading towards their rendezvous; it was Keith's Dad.

Panic set in; what were they to do? What if they were to race back down the hillside, but not get there in time? They would then have to do a u-turn and make their way back in the dark! They reckoned that if they ran back down, they could do it in 5 minutes; so off they sped, like the wind. So far so good! Nearly there!

They could see the car parked up with the lights on, but nobody got out so the engine was probably still running. Would they make it? Not far now; a little further and they'll surely see us, but no; the car began to move off, back onto the road and away, back towards the direction from whence it came. What now?

They were totally isolated, not a soul in sight; not even a sound, apart from that of the hapless pairs panting and gasping for breath. Their only option now was to start walking the nine and a half miles home; they finally reached an agreement and resolved that the safest route would be to go by road; it was longer, but they didn't want to risk getting lost in the hills, in the pitch black.

It seemed that they had been walking for an age, when during that time, a car pulled up and offered them a lift; it happened that they had walked half way. Luckily, the driver was going to a pub in the village where they were staying, and dropped them off there. Heaven knows what reception they found as they walked through the door; probably: you took your time, where the (dickens) have you been? Serves you right for not being there on time! Are you hungry?

Keith who had many family holidays in Cornwall and so knew that part of the country very well, used to talked enthusiastically about the villages, country pubs and old fashioned post offices; of the stone bridge over the stream in Tregony; the country lanes, clear blue seas, beautiful sandy beaches and the fresh air.

It sounded great! So we said why don't we go there next summer for our holidays? We were all excited, and so agreed that we should all go together without any adults; we were all in our early 20's, but what we meant was, without parents. It was decided that we rent a farmhouse for eight of us at £100 for the week, near St. Austell.

By the summer of 1976 there hadn't been any rain since March, the weather was rapidly warming up and a heat wave was predicted; temperatures would reach into the 90's F.

About a week before our holiday we all got together to discuss the journey.

Of the original eight, three dropped out because they had all met new girlfriends; they were: Alan Deverill, Steve Duke and my brother Jimmy; so that left five of us: Me, Keith West, Robert Pile (Taffy) , Mark Foster and Robert Duke. Keith wanted to leave late on Friday night to arrive in the morning, so he borrowed his Dad's 2 Litre Capri, loaded up and left just after 11pm with Mark and Taffy.

Robert and I decided to set off at 12noon the next day in the Austin A35 (PBH 498D). We made lots of stops along the way, because it was a long drive and all on 'A' roads, there were no motorways in the West-country then, but no matter how many times we stopped, or for how long, we always managed to find ourselves amongst the same cars and caravans going the same way.

We were averaging speeds of around 50mph, and arrived in St. Austell at the prearranged time of 8pm to meet the others at a pub in the town. After a short rest and a good old chinwag about the journey we set off to find the farmhouse, and when we thought we were close by, we called in to a local pub for directions.

As we entered all went quiet as the regulars turned and stared at us; it wasn't quite as bad as the pub scene from 'Werewolves of London' though, I just think that five lads strolling in with London accents took them by surprise. I suppose we must have appeared strange looking to those country folk, but they needn't have worried, because we were all country boys at heart.

When we got to the farmhouse it was still light and warm, with the sun still shining. A dusty track from the road led up to a large six bed roomed, typical West Country house, surrounded by barns and out buildings, set in amongst acres of land; the place was exactly how we imagined it would be. We couldn't believe our eyes. We got inside and had a wander around; it was wonderful.

What struck us most was the country kitchen with the huge walk-in larder, which also contained meat hooks. We were definitely going to enjoy our stay here. The next day we were up and out. There was so much to do in Cornwall and we wanted to do it all. Everything was so beautiful there; we went to lots of fishing villages, beaches and towns; we hired a boat to go mackerel fishing and even went horse riding.

On Wednesday we went to Perranporth in North Cornwall; it was fish and chips for dinner (midday is dinnertime to us) then on to the beach for the rest of the day, where we all got sunburnt. In the late afternoon we played crazy-golf, then off to the pub for a pint and a game of darts; a perfect end to a perfect day.

Going abroad is okay, but if the weather's good I thoroughly recommend Cornwall, especially if you have good company. Caravan, Castle, Hotel or Tent; take your pick! There's no worry of passports, foreign money or checking-in. You're guaranteed a decent cup of tea, proper English food and a good pint; and everyone speaks English! Well they did then!

On what day Taffy and I met the girls (Christine and Jackie) I can't remember exactly, but I do remember us taking them out to a country pub, taking photos and just having a great time. Me and Taff went back to Cornwall later on in the year to see the girls, and they came to see us the following year.

Taff, Jackie, Christine and me

Christine and I kept in contact by letter, and also, which was only once or twice, by phone, because neither of us had a phone in the house, so on those occasions we pre-arranged a time and day for me to call her neighbour (Stenalees 391) from a callbox at my end. I sort of lost contact with Taffy the following year, seeing him only occasionally. I suppose we were all getting older and pursuing different interests.

Taff loved Rock 'n' Roll, particularly Buddy Holly; he had all his records, played guitar and even wore the same glasses, he was a real rocker, and so gravitated towards likeminded people. Even so, we'd meet up now and then to take out a couple of girls, socialise or go swimming. His easy going nature, and pleasant sense of humour combined with his infectious laugh, made him hugely popular with everyone, and he always had a pretty girl on his arm.

The first time we met Taff, was when he turned up from Wales at 'juniors' school, and became an instant hit.

Poor Taffy. His problems started two or three years earlier when he fell in love and married a rich girl from Ascot, however, he was never really accepted by the snooty parents. The newlyweds bought a house together in Ledgers Road, Chalvey, but had problems from the start. I suspect it wasn't grand enough for her!

Taffy worked hard and tried his best but, sadly for him, it wasn't enough, and she ran back to her parents leaving him alone in the marital home. We all knew he was cut up about it, and even more so when his wife filed for divorce. Taff would always phone Keith if he wanted to meet up with us, because he was the only one with a phone, but on the fateful day that Taff killed himself, he couldn't get hold of him.

It transpired that, Taffy had phoned Keith from Slough and left a message asking him to meet him in the Nags Head. When Keith didn't show up, Taff continued walking on (he walked everywhere, I don't think he ever got behind the wheel of a car) up to the Britwell to see some of his other, newfound friends, where, apparently, they all had a drink whilst discussing Taffy's predicament. Unfortunately, the fact is that they let Taffy leave the house late at night whilst drunk and very upset.

His decapitated body was recovered from the mainline track below Dover Road Bridge, on the Trading Estate, and in his possession was the decree absolute. Tragic! Tragic! Tragic! A record of death by misadventure was registered on the 24th June 1978 and on the 29th a service was held prior to his cremation, in the chapel at Slough crematorium which was packed out; he was just 24 years old! God rest his soul.

My brother Jim told me that he had picked Taffy up in Windsor and given him a lift into Slough some months ago, and that Taffy didn't stop talking about the holiday in Cornwall, Jimmy was envious because he should have been with us, but I felt happy knowing that Taff had enjoyed the holiday as much as the rest of us.

*

Despite 1977 being the year of the Queen's Silver Jubilee, with all the pomp and celebration that was going on; it was to me - to use the term Her Majesty uttered in 1992, in her reference to that year - my *Annus Horribilis*. It felt this way to me, because, among other things, I had changed direction at work and was studying electronics to enhance my electrical skills.

IT and electronic controls were the buzz words then; labour saving machines were being developed and installed that could do the work of ten people on the factory assembly lines, so that in the years ahead less time would be spent at work, leaving more time for leisure pursuits.

It was this change of direction, which I pursued for a couple of years that upset my equilibrium. I think it's because of certain events, that you sort of lose your way, which causes you to reach out and search for some normality. Anyway, I persevered with the electronics but it was hopeless;

I just couldn't grasp it. The whole concept was alien to me and evolving at a rate of knots. I felt like a fish out of water and it was making me miserable. This period marked a turning point in my life and it took me a while to come through it.

Slough was the first town in the country to have one of the new purpose-built 'sports centres' that would soon appear in every town up and down the country. I disliked it from the outset, because firstly, not only did it look like an aircraft hanger, but also because inside there was no natural daylight or ventilation. Secondly, they destroyed Montem recreation grounds, along with the iron gates and railings and the boating lake, to build this huge ugly structure with its acres of car parking.

The upsides though, was that everyone would be much fitter, and lead a healthier life style pursuing one or another kind of physical activity that it would provide; gone would be the days of work until you drop. I felt that things were changing too quickly in the name of 'modernisation'. The Slough Karate Club for example, gave up their training gym at the local church hall, and relocated in the new sports centre as soon as it opened, but it wasn't to last.

First of all, subscriptions doubled, then it became too big, and then the senior grades wanted to form a committee to enable them to take over the running of the club. Finally there were splits which led to the club's eventual demise, with each of the instructors going off to form their own clubs in, wait for it, church halls, community centres and school halls. There's probably a moral there somewhere!

*

My dad died at a relatively young age, in May 1976 at only 56 years of age, yet despite all the hardship he had caused my mum, she stayed at his bedside till the end. I wonder if that had something to do with why 1977 marked a turning point in my life. I'd told Christine that I didn't want to be in a relationship; that I needed some time to myself. What was I thinking of? I'd lost my way; like a cork bobbing about in the vast ocean; she was a lovely girl, we'd have made a fine couple.

In her last letter she wrote: ...Father had left the door of the budgie cage open while he was cleaning it, and the little perisher flew off. Mother said: 'I expect that's the end of him; we won't be having any more pets' I expect if you tell Taff that he'd say good job. I'm feeling a bit down in the dumps. I think it's because you have gone back, I hope you are feeling the same way about me, because if you are it would make me feel better. I hope I haven't said anything so far to upset you, because I want you to continue to write. If I have please let me know, then I will try to explain what I really mean, and put it right.

I still have the letters in their envelopes, complete with their eight and a half penny postage stamp.

At the age of 26 years, instead of taking time out to reflect on my life, I feel now that I should have been in a serious relationship, if not married with children on the way, then my mum would have seen them, which was something she'd longed for; Oh what a wonderful thing hindsight is! Contrary to expectation though, 'time and tide wait for no man'; to coin another of my mum's expressions.

Taff dying so young was a wrench and, unhappily, just added to my adverse circumstances. It didn't help that my mum wanted to move from 104, the house that I loved, to another area in Slough where I felt totally alienated. I hated it there! I was becoming consumed in a downward spiral of negativity and had to break the cycle somehow. How could I apply the brakes to this impasse?

The easiest way to begin to do that was to stop doing the job that I now found myself engaged in! It happened like this: I heard the anticipated knock on my door at 7am, got out of bed and went over to the open window; the sun was shining and it was a beautiful day. There was my workmate looking up smiling; 'come on, get out of bed; we'll be late' he said. At which I replied: 'I'm finished! It's over! I'm not coming back to work! I'll be in later to hand in my notice.'

Having enough money to tide me over for a while I decided not to look for another job for at least 6 months. Thinking that by then I should have a clearer idea of what I wanted to do, but in the meantime I would keep myself busy by hiring a petrol mower to cut mine and my neighbours lawns. It was the middle of summer; the grass was growing rapidly and I soon became inundated with further requests to mow lawns and cut hedges, etc. For a small fee, you understand.

Now I could spend more time at the stables, after riding in Cornwall had awakened my interest in horses once again. I got on well with Mrs Peters, who ran the 'Stoke Poges' riding school at the farm, and had had a crush on her daughter Sylvia, who had taught me to ride over ten years before, but who, unfortunately, had left to get married by this time. What rotten timing!

Mrs P knew how interested I was in horses, and offered me a job, but at the time I was happy just to help out. I would take out the rides on a weekend, and generally just spend time there during the week, whenever I was at a loose end.

Seamus worked at the farm and I quickly became friends with him; he reminded me of Taffy in a way. Reg Rough owned the farm, and his brother Jim and wife Pat would come and stay at weekends, and we all became friends. We had barbecues and Christmas parties, and that period marked another turning point in my life, but this time it was a turn for the better.

The out-of-town Wexham Park District Hospital, newly built and completed in 1967 to replace all the local hospitals in each town, was a stone's throw from the farm. All of its porters and many of its student nurses, who were trained on the ward as well as in the purpose built on-site school, were recruited locally.

A social club with a disco or another type of entertainment on the weekend, which, incidentally, was very well attended, was provided for the staff and also for the use of the local residents, so that's where we from the farm used to socialise. Sadly this is no more! Gone is the social club – bulldozed to provide extra parking places for the original, massively expanded and overflowing car park – and gone also are the locals; all replaced by migrant workers from all over the world; I wonder why?

*

A couple of years ago my son broke his leg (femur) and spent three months in traction on the children's ward; most of the time he was the only white kid in there, and nearly all the staff, security, porters, surgeons and consultants were Black, Oriental, Asian or Eastern European.

The 'two visitors to a bed' rule was frequently ignored, with sometimes three generations of the same family around one bed eating prepared hot meals, changing babies' nappies and so on.

From visitors incessantly speaking loudly on mobile phones in a foreign tongue, to mothers sleeping on their children's beds fully clothed and with their shoes on, you'd be hard pressed to imagine this was a scene in a children's ward in an English hospital. It was diabolical!

On asking one nurse, with grubby cuffs, why she didn't observe the 'no long sleeves' rule for hygiene purposes, she replied: 'it's because of my religion'! There were antiseptic dispensers everywhere, strategically placed, for visitors entering or leaving the ward, which were routinely ignored. I just prayed that my son didn't pick up a serious infection through his open wounds, whose dressings had to be changed twice a day.

I'd visit my son every evening and stay with him until he was ready to go to sleep. He was eventually taken out of 'bed' traction and wore a sort of brace that enabled him to get out of bed and into a wheelchair. This was good for him because it meant that I could wheel him around the hospital as far as the exit doors and sometimes sit just outside. During these little excursions we would visit the randomly placed refreshment bays where he would have a drink and a steak pie etc. On one occasion there were two young men standing there with their mate, who looked quite ill; they had rushed him over from Aylesbury. When we began talking to them, they told us that two of them were in the fire brigade and one was a copper; they were struck by the amount of foreigners, patients and staff, in the hospital and added that they hadn't seen one white face until we showed up; I replied that "this was 'multicultural' Slough". They questioned why it was so necessary for the hospital to employ immigrants when there are masses of our own people unemployed and I'm afraid that I didn't know the answer to that either. What I am sure about is that, we once had a system that encouraged school leavers to take up medical training, for a career in the NHS which turned out a constant stream of newly trained doctors and nurses. It's so simple, it's brilliant! It's not rocket science; we have over a million unemployed youngsters so there's no shortage of people to fill those situations is there?

Now where was I?

Oh yes!

I remember…

…Parents were encouraged to stay overnight and were provided with a temporary bed placed next to their children, in that way the parent could attend to their child without constantly calling for nurse. At first, I would call the nurse for a blanket, a drink or a 'bottle' because he couldn't get out of bed, then after a while they would say: 'you know where it is'; so I became an unpaid ward assistant.

Now then, I didn't mind and was quite amazed at their lax attitude. I wondered if this had always been the case in the children's ward; would matron have allowed it in her day.

When initially admitted into hospital, the doctor carried out a careful examination and several tests, concluding that this was a 'comminuted fracture' where the bone had broken in four places but hadn't penetrated the skin. I was told that they couldn't operate until the swelling had gone down, so he was kept in bed under observation for a few days.

When they were satisfied he was ready, they gave me an approximate date for the operation but didn't explain the procedure. I went with him to the operating theatre where he was anesthetised; him saying: "don't worry dad, it'll be alright" as he became subdued; leaving me in emotional turmoil.

On leaving the theatre, the consultant called me over to his office to explain to me the operation they had decided on. Well this was not the right time to show me detailed operating procedure that would involve cutting him and inserting pins. The alternative was traction, which I opted for. MISTAKE!

As a result of my poor decision, my son became a long term (3 months) patient but was given a nice position by the window, and adored by all the nurses; well he did become part of the furniture.

Regrettably, the traction alternative resulted in him returning to theatre many more times, each being an agonising and traumatic experience for me, that didn't get any easier. It was so upsetting. I felt overcome with it all and needed a nurse to take me back to his ward where I waited to be called back. I became very rundown and developed a sever throat infection that lasted several weeks and permanently damaged my vocal cords. So I say to anyone who finds themselves in a similar situation "don't be pressured into being a 'trendy' parent. Stay in the ward"! I think that it's wrong to ask the parents to over indulge and then not give them due warning of what to expect. Had my options been explained to me clearly, and in good time, I would have, without doubt, agreed to have the pins inserted and he would have been discharged in two weeks.

Several years later as my son was approaching 19 he was having ongoing problems because the traction hadn't worked. The fracture had healed well enough but with slight angulation and shortening (18mm) it was causing him to drop his pelvis. This length discrepancy was also causing him headaches, lower back pain and discomfort in the ankle. As the condition worsened, he was offered orthopaedic surgery at the Nuffield Hospital in Oxford. which involved a surgical break, realignment and lengthening.

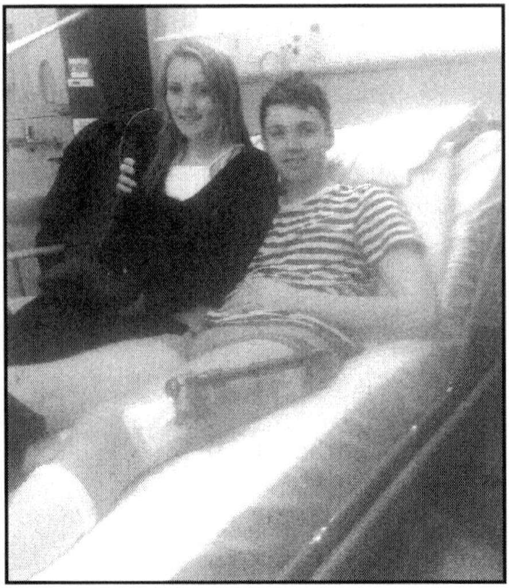

Kelly Anne and Joe showing lengthening iron-work

This operation took place in January 2015 and has been a complete success thanks to the amazing, kind and professional staff of the Limb Recontruction Team under Mr David Stubbs; with special thanks to llizarov Nurse Specialist Marion (maz) Sutherland.

*

The end of my 'horrible year' couldn't come soon enough, so on New Year's Eve 1977 I saw the old year out and the new in with great and eager anticipation knowing and feeling that this was a landmark turning point in my life. My life was beginning to move again in a positive direction. My childhood hero, Superman, was to be released for the first time, as a full length feature film; made locally at Pinewood Studios; a film that was to help to rejuvenate the ailing British Film industry.

'Grease' was released earlier its feel good effect was long lasting, and alongside this, the hugely popular, long running TV sitcom 'Happy Days' added to the celebration of the idealized vision of the mid to late 1950's.

'Jim'll fix it' (dare I mention his name?); 'The Muppet Show' and the 'Rockford Files' just to name a few of my many favourites were being shown on the telly. One of my all time favourite records was 'Hit me with your rhythm stick' by Ian Dury and the Blockheads which was being regularly played on the radio along with other greats from the Boomtown Rats who hailed the beginning of the Punk Rock era.

On the work scene I was managing to keep busy; returning to agency work with Manpower kept me in full time employment although the amount of good jobs were thinning out, because by this time British industry was on the wane, and factories were laying off people and closing down at a frightening rate. Where were they all to go? Probably, as was thought then, into IT, or the Sports and leisure industry!

It was a very nice year; I was back working doing the job I loved, and getting well paid for it, then after work spending time at the farm riding and looking after the horses, which was especially enjoyable during the warm summer evenings. Seamus became my best friend and we spent all our free time together, going out and about having great fun and chatting up as many girls as we could meet.

As the winter months approached, in what became known as the "Winter of Discontent" it became very cold; the snow fell early, and remained well into the next year, becoming the coldest since 1962–63.

The economic and political turmoil that was going on in the country at that time though, didn't affect me in the least. Elsewhere there were widespread strikes by local authority trade unions demanding larger pay rises for their members, because the Labour government of James Callaghan sought to hold a pay freeze to control inflation.

Previously, in 1976, Callahan had gone cap in hand to the International Monetary Fund for a £2.3bn loan to combat the rampant inflation at that time. This was perceived as a humiliation for a former imperial power and the nadir of the post-war economic decline.

Meanwhile, rubbish piled up, factories closed, picket lines blockaded hospital entrances, lorry drivers and gravediggers went on strike and the bodies piled up; at one point it was suggested that burials at sea might be a solution to the backlog

The strikes though, according to the polls, had a profound effect, helping to pave the way for Margaret Thatcher's 1979 General Election success. Things could have been so different for Callaghan's government, had he called an early election, because although dominated by the troubles with a minority in the House of Commons, by the autumn of 1978 most opinion polls showed Labour ahead, with the probability of winning him a second term in office until autumn 1983.

The general election was eventually called for the 3rd May 1979 off the back of the 'Winter of Discontent' producing a landslide victory for the Conservative Party, led by Margaret Thatcher, whose campaign had focused on a pledge to control inflation, reduce the power of the unions, and to gain support from traditional Labour and Liberal voters, and first-time voters.

This strategy combined with the employment of the advertising agency Saatchi & Saatchi resulted in an overall swing of 5.2%, the largest since 1945, beating the Labour government of James Callaghan with a parliamentary majority of 43 seats, and giving the country its first ever female Prime Minister.

The new government embodied the hopes and aspirations of its new leader, who on arriving at 10 Downing Street, paraphrased the "Prayer of Saint Francis":

Where there is discord, may we bring harmony. Where there is error, may we bring truth. Where there is doubt, may we bring faith. And where there is despair, may we bring hope.

Once comfortably installed at No.10, Mrs T. set about closing or selling off state owned companies and withdrawing subsidies to others determined to reverse what she perceived as the sheer haste of national decline; emphasising deregulation, particularly of the financial sector, and championing the growth of the flexible labour markets.

The year progressed very nicely, pretty much in the same vein as the one before, as well as being full of many positive uplifting events. I'd bought my first continental quilt 'duvet', they were all the rage. How posh! Out went all the old heavy blankets. The transformation was unbelievable; the warmth without the weight! In came double glazing, and gas central heating. Gone were the days of ice on the inside of the windows. How did we ever manage? My work situation was improving and moving in the right direction, and as a consequence, I was feeling much keener now to make future plans, especially as I had met (9th April 1979) a new girlfriend, so my thoughts were on buying a house and settling down.

I bought my first work van, a Morris Marina, registered self-employed as a sole trader on the 7th January 1980 and continued to work hard to earn a deposit for a mortgage. I got off to a good start but began to struggle as Mrs T. true to her manifesto promise, began to tackle inflation which reached the dizzy height of 22% that year. She also changed trade union laws in an attempt to reduce the strikes which had blighted Britain for so many years. As a result of her policies many factories, shipyards and coal pits were forced to close resulting in 3,000,000 unemployed by January 1982. The plus side though, was that strikes were at their lowest level since the early 1950's, and inflation fell below 10% by the turn of 1982. Very soon though, due to massive losses in our strong manufacturing base, notably in heavy industry, particularly in the north, Britain no longer could call itself the workshop of the world. These were dire times, giving the Tories an approval rating of just 25%. What was happening to our great country: we, who had spawned the Industrial Revolution?

By 1980, we had become used to terror attacks by the IRA on mainland Britain when one evening on the news, there fully televised for all to see, were men totally clothed in black and heavily armed, clambering over the balconies of very posh London buildings. Then in an instant, there were explosions, billowing smoke and the men dissappearing inside. How could this be happening in a London street, on a beautiful sunny day?

As we watched the events unfold in front of us, we were motionless with open mouths and in complete silence. Dogs were barking, people were screaming and gunshots could be heard. I think we were shocked to see this in real time. Who were these men in black?

Mrs Thatcher was not long into her premiership when she was faced with this, the Iranian embassy siege 30th April to 5th May 1980. She was to prove to the country, and anyone else for that matter, what she was made of after a group of six heavily armed men led by Oan Ali Mohammed stormed the Iranian embassy in South Kensington, taking 26 hostages, one of them PC Trevor Lock.

After 45 minutes exactly, three shots were heard from inside the embassy, Oan announced that a hostage had been killed, and the rest would die in 30 minutes unless his demands were met; a body was then thrown out into the street. Home Secretary Willie Whitelaw, was rushed back to Whitehall from a function he had been attending in Slough roughly 20 miles away, arriving 19 minutes after the shots had been reported.

The Metropolitan Police Commissioner requested that control of the operation be handed over to the Army, Whitelaw relayed the request to Thatcher, and the prime minister agreed immediately. He was briefed on the SAS plan and told to expect that up to 40% of the hostages would be killed in an assault.

The two SAS teams, Red and Blue were ordered to begin their

simultaneous assaults. One group lowered a stun grenade through the skylight, to coincide with the abseiling teams detonating explosives to gain entry to the building through the second-floor windows. The first wave of soldiers smashed their way into the embassy followed by a second wave.

As the soldiers emerged onto the first-floor landing, PC Trevor Lock tackled Oan to prevent him attacking the SAS men. Oan, still armed, was quickly identified and shot dead by one of the soldiers. Meanwhile, at the rear of the building, further SAS teams began evacuating hostages, down the stairs towards the back door of the embassy.

One of two terrorists, identified by an SAS man, hiding amongst the hostages produced a hand grenade; the soldier didn't shoot for fear of hitting hostages, but pushed the terrorist to the bottom of the stairs, where two other soldiers shot him dead.

During the 17-minute raid, the SAS rescued all but one of the remaining hostages, and killed five of the six terrorists. The SAS was largely unknown owing to the covert nature of its operations but because the raid was broadcast, live at peak time, on a bank holiday Monday evening and was viewed by millions of people, the SAS was now a household name, not least in the 'Trotter' household (Only Fools and Horses TV program); 'He who dares wins, Rodney; He who dares'. Now follow that if you can?

*

My first year in business, although getting off to a good start, was abysmal; we, as a country, were going down the pan! There was a big shock looming that nothing could have prepared us for, as events unfolded outside the Dakota building in New York that would put things into perspective. I don't think there could have been anything right then, at that moment, to eclipse the news that John Lennon had been shot and killed by a crazed gunman on the steps at the entrance of his apartment (10:50 pm, 8th December 1980).

The New Year, for me, work wise, got off to a slow start and remained that way for the rest of the year, so I resorted to sub-contract work with builders and so on to keep myself busy. Meanwhile, Margaret Thatcher's popularity was on the slide as a consequence of the recession, rising unemployment and her economic policies, giving her a record low approval rating of just 23%. To add to her woes the "stop and search laws" recently introduced, were beginning to cause unrest.

The "sus laws" as they were commonly referred to, were introduced to give the Police new powers, under the 1824 Vagrancy Act, to stop, search and arrest anyone based on only a 'reasonable suspicion' that an offence had been committed. "Any person found in a public place, and suspected of going with the intent to commit an arrestable offence shall be deemed a rogue and vagabond, and if found guilty would be liable for up to three months imprisonment" In order to bring a prosecution, the police had to establish two things: first, that the defendant had been acting suspiciously, and secondly, that there was intent to commit a criminal offence. Furthermore, two witnesses were required to substantiate the charge, which was usually two police constables patrolling together.

The laws were mainly implemented in areas that had large ethnic minorities of Afro-Caribbean decent, such as Slough, and therefore, were disproportionately applied to the Black community, causing widespread resentment amongst young black men; sparking off riots, first in Brixton, and then in a dozen other towns and cities around the country. I can understand how some would find this new law resentful because me and two other friends were stopped, as we walked in Slough on a warm summers evening, for no reason at all. We were not against being asked questions by the police but it was the manner in which they carried it out. It was like a scene from the 'Sweeney'. An unmarked car screeched up, all doors flew open and the coppers ran towards us, put us against the fence and began to frisk us. It was laughable! They then jumped back into their car and sped off!

Although I and many of my friends were stopped and searched, we didn't feel that these new powers were directed specifically towards us; we actually thought that they were over the top and ridiculous. Huge resentment though, rose in the Asian community, who felt isolated and vulnerable to racist attack as the Police carried out their new laws to question people about their immigration status.

Slough didn't actually see the worst of the riots, but there was a sense of unease nevertheless; it didn't feel nice and I didn't like the direction our country was going in.

Enoch Powell had warned, years before, of the dangers of a "racial civil war" in Britain when he predicted racial tension arising from the influx of large numbers of people from the third world. It appears that the political elite still don't get it. The growth of immigration has now reached an annual total of 641,000, the majority from Asia and Africa.

The situation can only get worse thanks to the chaos in Europe and the vast exodus of migrants across the Mediterranean.

In this same year, Defence Secretary John Nott's infamous Defence White Paper at a time of domestic recession, announced massive cuts for the Royal Navy proposing a reduction of a fifth of its 60 destroyers and frigates, with plans to concentrate almost solely on Britain's role in NATO. By 1982 there were signs of economic recovery, and although inflation was down to 8.6% from a high of 18%, unemployment was still too high at over 3 million for the first time since the1930's, making the Thatcher government highly unpopular. Moreover, Nott's short-sighted Defence cuts marked the end of his career, as the very crisis that his review had ruled out took place.

The Argentinean ruling military junta, needing a victory, invaded the Falkland Islands in April, with the intention of retaking the island before the 150th anniversary of British rule.

Included in the general reduction in size of the Royal Navy was the planned withdrawal of the last of the Antarctic Supply vessels, HMS Endurance. The Argentines interpreted this, and the 1981 British Nationality Acts aim to replace full British citizenship of Falklanders with a more limited version, as a lack of British interest in those islands. They were confident that the British would be in no sort of shape to put up a fight in the midst of recession, cuts and the domestic unrest, added to the fact that the islands lay over 8,000 miles away in Argentinean territory.

This must have appeared as a blessing to Margaret Thatcher, who could now parade as a 'Churchillian' figure with a 'bulldog spirit, totally surprising the nation by assembling a Task Force in record time; it was an amazing feat of mobilisation.

Within less than a week a British Task Force had set sail to retake the islands! Two cruise liners for example, the QE11 and the Canberra were refitted in a matter of a few days, and headed off with troops and helicopters for the nearest British airbase at the Ascension Island; an 11 day trip 4000 miles away in the South Atlantic Ocean, midway between the UK and the Falklands.

The British Government imposed a 200-mile exclusion zone around the Islands on the 26th April to prevent Argentine reinforcements and supplies reaching the Islands from the mainland, and warned Argentina that any ship or aircraft representing a threat to the task force would be attacked and destroyed. This allowed our troops to land virtually unhindered. The landings took place on the 21st May in San Carlos, on the opposite side of the island to the capital Port Stanley, from where our elite units such as the Para's and the Marine's fought their way across the island, meeting with mainly weak resistance, and heavily outnumbered by an inexperienced Argentinean army with a poor morale.

After 3 weeks of fighting and the loss of 250 men, the British took the Argentine surrender, whose losses were 746. The prisoners, who numbered 12,278, were assembled at Stanley airfield, and then repatriated back to Argentina on ships such as the Norland and the Canberra. Amazingly, there were only 3 civilian deaths. The conflict was widely covered by the print and broadcast media, and consequently, avidly received by the British public; who incidentally, had never heard of the islands. In fact when questioned, most thought they were somewhere off Scotland in the Outer Hebrides.

After all the awful events of the past few years, were the fortunes of our great country about to take a turn for the better? Maggie had become a national hero and there was resurgence in pride and patriotism. Here was someone that was prepared to stand up and fight for our country at last. I am sure that I and thousands more switched to the Tories for the first time in our lives to support her and show our appreciation.

*

By the middle of 1983, through diligent hard work, I had amassed the princely sum of around £5,000 and was finally in a position to buy my own house. Being 32 years old though, I was getting near the age where I would have been too old to get a mortgage. That sounds a strange thing to say these days, but back then, 25 years was the maximum repayment term, because you expected to pay off your mortgage long before retirement.

Very few people had bank accounts as wages were made up at the end of each week in cash, and were received in a pay-packet; a 3x4 inch envelope with a window, stapled at the top to prevent fraud. It was the highlight of the week, and most eagerly awaited by employees across the country each Friday afternoon. As a consequence of the this very fine arrangement, Building Societies, who paid a better interest rate than Banks, were the preferred choice for savers hoping to purchase their own property.

If you had, for example saved with the very popular post office as one of their 'savings account' holders; or in my case, the Trustee Savings Bank (TSB) you were required to transfer your money to a Building Society and continue saving with them for at least a year before being considered for a loan. A 10% deposit was needed, along with proof of earnings before your loan could be initiated; then subject to a survey of the property in question, the process of your mortgage was activated.

I was quite interested in living in the town centre, and so settled for a large four bed roomed Victorian townhouse with a basement. It was a beautiful, original dwelling with a rateable value of £203, and an asking price of £22,500, that just needed some repair work carried out, a complete rewire and gas central heating.

From the outside it didn't look that big but once inside it was like the 'Tardis' with its high ceilings, three levels and large basement (formerly servants quarters) and wide staircase, it was much roomier than anywhere I'd lived previously.

When buying your own home there were two things to consider, the mortgage repayments and the rates, then in addition, of course, were the running and maintenance costs. Simple! Just make sure that you only buy a house you can afford, which is pure common sense really, then providing that you can hold on to your job, you had made it onto the first rung of the property ladder. It was a lot easier and less expensive up until the mid 1980's, and most people who bought their own houses usually lived in them for life.

The one-bedroom flats and starter homes are recent phenomena, precisely because of the massive property price boom since that time, pricing most mid-range earners out of the possibility of owning an average 3 bed semi. The value of my first house for example, had increased by over ten-fold in eighteen years. From £22,500 in 1984, to £250,000 by 2002.

Once I took possession of my property I began restoration work immediately. The basement was uninhabited and so boarded up on the outside, and on the inside there was no sign of access to it. Some investigative work from the outside into the cellar led to a large room 18ft x 12ft with a fire place.

Adjoining it was a coal-hole under the front footpath still containing about 3 hundredweight of coal. The ceilings were down and there were only a few remnants of what used to be a wooden floor; most of the plaster was gone, but amazingly there were the remains of the servant's bells with all the pulley wires still attached which I later discovered ran along the joists under the floor, to all the rooms of the house. As me and my brother Jim ventured under the house with a couple of torches we found another door on the far side, leading into another small room which we surmised, due to the hooks and shelves, to be a cloak-room or larder. In that same room was a broken down old staircase leading up to, yes! A blanked off small doorway.

We roughly paced out where that doorway would correspond to the inside of the house, where we found a blank wall decorated and skirted in keeping with the rest of the hall way. There was only one thing to do! Go back into the basement and punch a hole through; and where lo and behold we found ourselves on the landing under the stairs! At the back of the house was a small kitchen with a fireplace, probably for a boiler, or small cooking range; opposite that was a single cold water pipe to an inside toilet. Then on to a Geyser for boiling water, above a cast-iron bath on legs covered with a board which, I was told by the previous residents, who became regular visitors and friends, doubled up as a table or work surface when the bath was not in use.

It really was a beautiful, solidly built house of 1888, which had remained un-modernised, and unspoilt by DIY. All the original doors, and sash windows with wooden shutters on the inside, cornices and corbels were in place, as were the gas mantles which had been capped off; probably in the 1950's. From the evidence of the electrical cables and fittings that were there, this was also when it was wired for electric lights, for I could see no traces of earlier electric cables.

By all accounts, Slough was a fledgling Victorian town; built up along the A4, London to Bath coaching road; early traders built their shops and their houses close to each other, usually within walking distance. My house was built for the Ironmonger and hardware store of the family traders called 'Rabbitts' who remained in the town well into the 1980's.

My long-term girlfriend at the time was desperate for us to live together and start a family after almost three years of courtship, but the exchange of contracts took forever (8 months) and she became impatient and lost confidence in me somewhere along the line saying that this house would never materialise, and that it would all come to nothing.

What could I do? I was furious! It was the cause of many ups and downs, and things were said that shouldn't have been said in the heat of the moment until we ultimately parted. She married soon after and had a child but that liaison was sadly destined to failure, and although we remained friends I felt that too much water had passed under the bridge;

it was all too late, and reconciliation would have been futile.

Completion was finally on the 4th January 1984; I had a new girlfriend and many more after but never settled down. I did have a great life in that house though, with lots of friends and a full social life. I became so attached to that house and the surrounding 'Victoriana' that I sometimes imagined how marvellous it would be, if one morning when I woke up, I could find myself magically transported back a hundred years to see how Slough really looked, worked and functioned all those years ago. I'd go to the library or the 'Slough Museum' to gather as much information as possible. Several books were published around that time, two of which: *SLOUGH A Pictorial History* by Judith Hunter & Isobel Thompson (ISBN 0-85033-777-1), and *Around Slough IN OLD PHOTGRAPHS* Collected by Judith Hunter and Karen Hunter ISBN 1-84015-028-9, I purchased and studied, remembering many of the numerous old buildings that were still standing when I was young.

Slough has been in decline for a long time. In fact, it started in the mid 1960's when the progressive 'modernist' town planners decided that our beautiful Victorian town was 'ugly' and old fashioned, so they set to work with the wrecking-ball. They were relentless!

As I remember it, some of the first buildings to go were 'King's astronomer' William Herschel's 'Observatory House' in Windsor Road, against a great public outcry, and the Crown Public House on the Crown corner. Next they drove that huge 'runway' of a road through the very heart of Slough, laying waste to everything in its path.

They continued with their destructive plans when they built the 'overbearing' Queensmere shopping centre; this signalled the demise of our traditional High Street. Most of my friends and neighbours have moved away because they couldn't stand to live, any longer, in a town that has become virtually unrecognisable from the one they grew up in.

Redevelopment on this scale has been strongly criticised by conservation groups. The Twentieth Century Society (C20) has stated that "tragically high quantities of good buildings have been demolished in Slough in recent years, including grand Art-Deco-styled factories by the likes of Wallis Gilbert and high-quality post-war offices. More are to come down as the town tries to erase its past and reinvent itself from scratch". Despite famously heckling Slough, John Betjeman's praise for the Town Hall's architecture as 'a striving for unity out of chaos' in 1948 has never been so relevant as today. C20 believes that the redevelopment of the Town Hall would be an act of vandalism to the civic centre and is supporting the Campaign to Save Slough's Heritage in their request for a review.

Our present Labour council believe that by continuing with their expensive vanity projects like the new Bus Station and the 'Curve' it will somehow magically revitalise what was once a vibrant and prosperous town, bringing with it a night time 'café-culture'. What a laugh and a total waste of money! Would you visit Slough in the evening for a night out?

Throughout the 1980's and 90's the council remained on their destructive course, intent on destroying all of Slough's historic past and have it replaced by office blocks. It was only when Slough went conservative, during Maggie's wave of popularity that the Victorian residential area where I bought my house managed to survive. Under the Labour council's current 'regeneration' plan the destruction continues; yet more and more of our older buildings are being reduced to rubble. They are replaced by massive glass buildings, dual carriage ways and multi-occupancy high rise residential 'termite heaps'. Their plan is to build a futuristic town where they can make better use of the land. One Victorian villa with a large garden could well make way for a new development that would house a hundred families. Who needs gardens? Green space is money! I am convinced that the demise of Old Slough High Street has been deliberate and that the Queensmere shopping centre will eventually replace it. Once they get to that stage in their plan, it will be too late but I'm afraid that all the wasted £millions will do nothing to improve things.

It is abundantly clear that from the outset, they charged headlong with gusto to modernise everything, in the vain effort to shake off every vestige of anything pre-1960; with eyes set on the new millennium no doubt?

*

Policemen's tunics began to disappear in favour of a blue version of the army jumper with elbow patches and shoulder badge numbers. God forbid they ever replace the policeman's helmet which is now the only part of their uniform that distinguishes them from the common security guard. Bus drivers and conductors had long given up their uniforms complete with military style peaked caps, as can be seen in 'On the Buses' (TV program) as did Postmen who can frequently be seen these days delivering the morning (or, should I say 'any-time-of-day') post in shorts.

Ambulance drivers now wear a type of overall instead of the once very smart uniform complete with cap that marked them out from all the other services. I bet it was the lefties plan to rid itself of anything that looked military, disciplined or reeked of authority; in the same way that the Police Force is now a police-service, or that the Fire Brigade is now a fire-service. Even the Queens Guard at Windsor Castle modernised by exchanging their rifle for a short stubby machine pistol; it looks ridiculous and out of place against their red tunic and bearskin.

The Fire Brigade swapped their traditional uniforms in the 1980's for a more practical waterproof outfit for obvious reasons which is understandable given the job that they do; retaining their cavalry twill for ceremonial purposes only.

Whilst contracted to the MOD at RAF Medmenham, just the other side of Marlow in Buckinghamshire in the late 1980's (which had changed its usage to a military Police training college), I happened to be there on the day of their passing-out parade. Whilst the cadets were preparing their uniforms (they looked identical to the civilian police except they were trained in fire arms, and carried a pistol). I opened the door to one of the dormitories and there stood half a dozen or so police constables in the full parade kit. I knew most of them, but to see them all together in full parade dress, looking a little nervous, but so proud, took me aback. I felt humbled and slightly intimidated for a minute or so, and then one of them said "how do we look?" I think I said something like "smart!" but really, I thought they looked magnificent. It's a pity we don't still have that presence on our streets today; we need it.

A few weeks later I was talking to an old boy in the queue at Boots the Chemist, and for some reason started to tell him that story. He was impressed, but said the coppers in his day, after the war were really tough; they were usually ex military, 6ft Guardsmen who stood for no nonsense, saluted their sergeant and addressed him as sir. That it was common practice when in a civil disturbance to use their cape as a weapon to control the offenders; the idea was to take hold of the bottom edge and swing, so that the metal buttons and chain on the collar made contact.

Christianity has been sidelined in state schools and, consequently, children are being brought up in an entirely profane environment, and if not corrected by their parents, many end up on the streets running wild, where drugs are commonplace, because it's their right to do so isn't it!

Yobs frequently hurl abuse and swear at policemen and in public; it's obscene! Don't you wish that the coppers of today weren't so docile? No need to carry a gun, but just able to administer a slap.

*

Throughout the 1980's I remember being genuinely fearful of a third world nuclear war being triggered by an itchy finger or in retaliation to incoming missiles from the Soviet Union. Honestly, watching Maggie, the unbending 'iron lady' and Reagan the 'Hollywood cowboy' on telly, escalate the cold war, made the threat of an all out war, and the end of the world, very real, and I wasn't alone in these feelings.

As the tensions mounted between the two 'superpowers' with us in the middle, nuclear paranoia settled into the minds of many people. In fact, one night, while asleep; I must have been feeling particularly edgy, after watching a film featuring missiles flying through space towards their target, with a simultaneous attack coming from the opposite direction, when I was awoken by the dreadful ugly roar of rocket engines; I leapt out of bed to look out of the window, and saw in the sky, the hideous glow from the nuclear missiles as they passed over the house. This was it! They've started it! We're only 20 miles from London; we're bound to get caught in the blast! My girlfriend, who was lying beside me reached up and pulled me by the arm, saying "come back to bed, it's a Jumbo jet". I waited for a while until I became fully awake, and could make out the cabin lights of the 2.30am Heathrow to New York flight as it lumber overhead just out of arms reach; it seemed very low and I had felt very scared, taking several minutes before getting back to sleep.

In 1983 a film was made called 'The Day After' which depicted how a nuclear war might be initiated, and as the title implies; the disastrous consequences. The threat of war was so real that I couldn't bring myself to watch the film until just recently, and as I had expected, from watching newsreel of the bombing of Hiroshima and Nagasaki, the scene was total carnage. Unlike conventional warfare, those that weren't caught in the initial blast began to die from the nuclear fallout.

It says in the film: you can't see it, you can't feel or taste it, but it is passing though you like an x-ray destroying every cell in your body. Which begs the question; what is the point of nuclear weapons that will potentially contaminate the soil, the rivers and all living organisms? No one wins in the end, and it all started because of inflated egos, power struggles and aggression! As the credits roll at the end of the film, there follows a grim epitaph:

The catastrophic events
you have just witnessed are,
in all likelihood, less severe
than the destruction
that would actually occur
in the event of
a full nuclear strike against
the United States.

It is hoped that the images
of this film inspire
the nations of this earth,
the people and their leaders,
to find the means to avert
the fateful day.

*

What was very real though was the threat of terrorism, which manifested itself in many ways; one among them being, the bombing of the Grand Hotel in Brighton during the 1983 Conservative Party Conference. The bomb was planted under the bath in his room, by Provisional Irish Republican Army (IRA) member Patrick Magee, a month earlier, during his stay on the weekend of 14-17th September. He had fitted the bomb with a timing device set to go off at 2:54 am on the 12th October, with the intention of assassinating Prime Minister Margaret Thatcher and her cabinet.

Five people were killed, including Sir Donald Maclean and his wife Muriel, who were in the room in which the bomb exploded. The wife of Norman Tebbit, Margaret was left permanently disabled, but mercifully, the bomb failed to kill Thatcher or any of her government ministers; and of thirty-four injured all left Royal Sussex County hospital and recovered. That is physically, at any rate? At around 4:00 a.m. she gave an impromptu interview to the BBC, saying that the conference would go on as scheduled, and at 8 a.m. Marks & Spencer kindly opened their doors early, to allow those who had lost their clothes in the bombing to get new ones.

She delivered her speech as planned, claiming that the bombing was "an attempt to cripple Her Majesty's democratically elected Government": not only that this attack has failed, but that all attempts to destroy democracy by terrorism will fail. Her coolness and Churchillian stoicism noted in the immediate aftermath of the attack, won universal admiration and approval. She was widely supported across the political spectrum and her popularity soared nationwide.

The next day, the Provisional IRA issued a statement claiming responsibility. Adding that 'Today we were unlucky, but remember we only have to be lucky once. You will have to be lucky always'.

On top of all what was happening in the 1980's, our country sank to a new low with the murder of PC Blakelock. Our unarmed policemen were the envy of the world, but by the time of the riots they proved to be woefully inadequate. Relationships between Black communities and the police had broken down across the country, and on the Broadwater Farm housing estate in Tottenham, violence broke out after a black woman died of heart failure during a police search of her home.

During the unrest that ensued, PC Blakelock, who was assigned to a unit of 10 constables and a sergeant, known as Serial 502 to protect fire-fighters, stumbled and fell, and was surrounded by a mob of around 50 people. He was hacked to death in a frenzied attack receiving over 40 cutting or stabbing wounds, eight of them to his head, caused by a machete or similar weapon in what looked like an attempt to sever his head.

Colleagues barged in to rescue PC Blakelock from the mob and dragged him, still alive, to relative safety, but his wounds were so severe, that as well as having a six-inch knife embedded up to the handle in the back of his neck, all attempts to resuscitate him proved hopeless.

The killing of an unarmed British Bobby in my opinion is the height of all evil, and the abomination of a democratic and peaceful civilization. Although the nation was horrified and shocked at this, it wouldn't be very long before they'd be grieving again for the young and pretty WPC Yvonne Fletcher.

She was part of a detachment of 30 officers, sent to St. James's Square to monitor a demonstration by Libyan dissidents opposed to the rule of Colonel Muammar Gaddafi. The Libyan embassy was in the hands of armed Gaddafi loyalists, the so called 'revolutionary committees' with the approval of the Libyan government. Then during the morning, and without warning, automatic gunfire was discharged from the windows of the Embassy into the anti-Gaddafi protesters, killing the unarmed WPC Fletcher and hitting several others.

What was our country coming to, where would it all end? Well we have a pretty good idea now don't we? It hasn't improved much has it? More to the point what is to be done about it, and what government has the courage to implement the legislation for change? My feeling is that the whole of society needs to be pulled up by the bootstraps, beginning with more disciplined behaviour in the home and at schools, combined with a more visible police presence in the neighbourhoods, tougher jail sentences, and capital punishment for murder.

Today, we face a much more dangerous and sinister threat in the form of Islamic State (IS) I think no one is safe and the attack could come from anywhere. I don't think we've seen this level of threat since the rise of Nazism in the 1930's.

The security services are arresting suspected terrorists every day. Hundreds are returning from Syria who have been trained and fought with IS and are battle hardened. In addition to this, we must stop people with terrorist connections coming to Britain; we are being flooded with jihadists.

If we were no longer members of the EU, we could clearly determine who comes into Britain and who can't, but at the moment, anyone with an EU passport - even criminals - can enter unhindered. This is a real threat. We must have secure borders, and put an end to unlimited immigration. The dream of free movement has hit the buffers.

*

Well into the 1980's now, things were looking up. The economy was strong, inflation was low and there was plenty of work, so despite now having a mortgage of £140/month, which seemed a lot at the time, I was able to buy a new work van. It was one of those Honda 2-strokes with the side loading door; a 'bun van' I used to call it. It wasn't really suitable for me though, because the engine was under the back floor and that meant I had to empty out the contents any time I needed to get to the engine. I think it was more suitable when used as a run-around delivery vehicle, so I exchanged it quite early for a Ford Escort van, which was a much better proposition all around, and also the preferred vehicle at the time for tradesmen like myself.

Because of the buoyant economy, there was money to be earned and burned, especially in the City. It was the age of the 'Yuppie' as portrayed by Harry 'loads o' money' Enfield. Credit companies couldn't get rid of their cards quick enough. It wasn't a case anymore of, 'could I please make an appointment to see a mortgage advisor?' It was, 'would you like a mortgage, and how much?' No confirmation necessary. Normal rules had flown out the window; it was obscene, this 'live now pay later' mentality. Spend, spend, spend, was the order of the day. One thing that hadn't changed though was the Carol Singers. Not the Salvation Army Band that played in the High Street or the local church choir singing in the street but a group of young kids singing carols at the door. I didn't believe that kids still did that sort of stuff these days. When we did it all those years ago I swore that I would always give the kids who came to my door, at least half-a-crown (2/-6d). I heard the familiar sound, opened the door and to my delight, there stood four of the sweetest kids singing out. "Where are you from" I asked? "Manor Park... Beaumont Road". "You're a long way from home, sing another carol while I fetch you some money". I stood behind the front door in my hallway to listen to them singing for a while, and then returned to give them a pound each. There little faces were a picture. That never happened again.

As I was growing up, I was staggered at the moral decline in America, the widespread illegal drug-taking and the free-love as depicted by long-haired hippie drop-outs, but what was scarier was, that it was said, that whatever happens in America is then replicated in the UK. Hence the expression: 'when America sneezes, we catch a cold'.

In 1964 Jane Deverson was asked by *Woman's Own* magazine to interview teenagers of the time. It revealed a generation of teenagers who didn't respect parents, slept together before marriage and didn't have strong Christian beliefs; they were indifferent towards the Monarchy and tended to ignore leaders.

Similarly, Richard Linklater's film 'Slacker' explored young adult characters who were more interested in philosophizing than settling with a long-term career and family.

At the time of Harry Enfield's 'loads 'o' money I met some 'Geordie' electricians like myself, who had come down from South Shields in the North East to find work in the 'prosperous south', namely, Slough; not a problem, plenty of work at three times what they were earning up North. Needless to say, they settled down here, but were homesick.

I found them to be very proud and patriotic; they loved their part of the country and travelled back every weekend. They would always invite me to go with them, an offer I jumped at, and as my own dad was from

Newcastle, I wanted to see it for myself, a sort of pilgrimage really. I wasn't disappointed. It was as they described, only better, but like they used to say, 'it's a great place to live, but there's no work'. Hay aye: (oh yeah).

Even though I now owned my own house and was independent, it wasn't home and never would be without a wife and children. The problem was that I had plenty of friends and girlfriends, and consequently, had neither the desire nor the inclination to change that situation; not just then anyway. In hindsight however, procrastinating in that way, personally, was probably a mistake. I would go home to my mum, where my brother still lived, for a hot meal at least twice a week, and all day Sunday, and mum would say 'you act as if this is your home' to which I would reply: 'this is my home, that other place is just a house'. Because our family was very close to our mum, perhaps due to the selfless way in which she brought us up, always putting her children first, very often going without food in order to feed us first, she was never to feel left out, or on her own as we got older. It was because of her sense of duty towards us that she was never abandoned in her later years.

My brother Jim told me recently that he had had several opportunities to strike out on his own, he was never short of female admirers, but declined to do so, due to this same sense of duty, until after my mum had died. That fateful day came in January 1987, which was the worst day of our lives, changing them irrevocably. The strange thing is that we knew she couldn't go on forever; after all, she was 76. Nevertheless, we were still unprepared.

Jim, I think, was affected the most, but he shortly found a young woman with the intention of settling down, had two children and is now happily married. I on the other hand had the travel bug, booking a skiing trip to Verbier, Switzerland the following month, then to Crete in the summer, and finally, at the end of the year, to Australia (bi-centenary year) and the far East for a couple of months from December 1987 to February 1988.

Eventually I returned from what turned out to be the holiday of a lifetime. In fact my mate (Merve the Swerve) had a tear in his eye as we boarded the British Airways flight from Bangkok to London. Once back home and returning to a normal routine again, the loss of my mum, and not being able to just pop in for a visit, began to build up. Everybody in our family shared that great sense of loss, and it doesn't get any easier. Equally though, we all feel her presence around us constantly, and that helps.

Anyway, life goes on as it must, and it was time now to get back into work. It was quite difficult to shake off the holiday mode though, especially with a suntan in February and the additional few pounds in body weight acquired due to the lack of activity and good food; and booze! Nevertheless, in the bar, after our first training session, with Mick and Adam at 'Bojangles', we told of our adventures, backed up with photos of all the magic that our trip entailed, and of all the beautiful Thai girls.

Mick and Adam were of the old school Karate training and veterans of the Slough Shotokan Club, which turned out some of the best karate men in the Southern region, so needless to say, the training was very tough. The highlight of the year being the annual pilgrimage to Enoeda Sensei's training camp at the Crystal Palace national sports centre. There would be Sensei's assistant Ohta 5th Dan, and three or four top guest instructors from Japan 6th Dan and above. The course was billed as an international residential event with full board accommodation at the on-site hostel, was hugely popular due to the infamous 'Shotokan Tiger' which of course was the name given to Sensei Enoeda, and ran until his death in 2003, receiving hundreds of students from far and wide. Great memories!

*

I had never been a political animal, when it came to voting, I had to look to my mum for advice, who said: "working class people are 'the salt of the earth' and we are what we are; no better than anyone else and no worse. Our health and happiness are most important, without them all the money in the world is worthless. You had better vote labour Son, because the Labour Party is for us" So there it is then, good sound advice, for a young 18 year old.

So off I went to the polling booth, still wet behind the ears, to put my cross firmly into the Labour box. It didn't mean 'toffee' did it? It was just a veneer of democracy to make us feel that we were having our say and making a difference, because all along, the plan was always to surrender our sovereignty, to become a mere member state of the 'brave new world' called the European Union. In fact decimal coinage was already in circulation, and although, running alongside our much loved 'imperial' currency, it would never actually replace it, would it? Something would surely turn up at the last minute and it would all have turned out to be a big bad mistake. There! We should never have gone along with it, and had nothing to do with it from day one. We had been told that it was about trade; a common market that would involve no loss of essential sovereignty. That's how Ted Heath sold it to us, and the majority of the electorate believed it.

The 1975 referendum was won in favour of staying in the common market, and the end of the UK was nigh. The insidious creep towards Euro-federalism was on, and in most people's eyes, inevitable. I believe that during the period between the early 1960's and until the present day, people have been turned off politics, because no matter who gets in, they were all hopeless, it's the same old story. They're all saying and doing the same thing; and to quote Nigel Farage of UKIP: "you can't put a cigarette paper between them". The reason for this electoral apathy? Is simple, its because the MP's we elect to Parliament are hamstrung by Brussels and have no real powers. So they can't faithfully represent us.

I've got to admit, I was one of the disillusioned masses of people who had given up on democracy; we were fast becoming EU citizens, including the Queen. We have this horrible metric toy-money, metric weights and measures and mass free movement of people across Europe (and the rest of the world) mainly to the UK, although we still measure distance in miles, still have the pint, even if the pubs are becoming extinct, and we still drive on the left; for now anyway. Is it any wonder that the British are losing their sense of national pride and social cohesion, not to mention the national faith of Christianity?

Political awakening

Reading Mrs Thatcher's Bruges speech of the 20th September 1988 opened my eyes, the extract below show why!

"Willing and active cooperation between independent sovereign states is the best way to build a successful European Community. To try to suppress nationhood and concentrate power at the centre of a European conglomerate would be highly damaging. Europe will be stronger precisely because it has France as France, Spain as Spain, Britain as Britain, each with its own customs, traditions and identity. But working more closely together does not require power to be centralised in Brussels or decisions to be taken by an appointed bureaucracy.

The Soviet Union, tried to run everything from the centre, learned that success depends on dispersing power and decisions away from the centre. Certainly we want to see Europe more united and with a greater sense of common purpose, but it must be in a way which preserves the different traditions, Parliamentary powers and sense of national pride in one's own country; for these have been the source of Europe's vitality through the centuries.

Some of the founding fathers of the Community thought that the United States of America might be its model, but the whole history of America is quite different from Europe.

People went there to get away from the intolerance and constraints of life in Europe. They sought liberty and opportunity; and their strong sense of purpose has over two centuries, helped create a new unity and pride in being American - just as our pride lies in being British or Belgian or Dutch or German.

The British Approach, believe it is not enough just to talk in general terms about a European vision or ideal. If we believe in it, we must chart the way ahead and identify the next steps. Let Europe be a family of nations, understanding each other better appreciating each other more, doing more together but relishing our national identity no less than our common European endeavour.

This approach does not require new documents: they are all there, the North Atlantic Treaty, the Revised Brussels Treaty, and the Treaty of Rome, texts written by farsighted men, a remarkable Belgian - Paul

Henri Spaak - among them.

It is to NATO that we owe the peace that has been maintained over 40 years. ...we cannot rely for ever on others for our defence, but that each member of the Alliance must shoulder a fair share of the burden."

Did you also know that:

The Single European Act of 1986 (SEA) was the first major revision of the Treaty of Rome with the objective of establishing a Single Market, closer union, with Qualified Majority Voting (QMV) and greater powers for the European Parliament.

Qualified Majority Voting is a method of making decisions in which each member state's vote is weighted enabling certain resolutions to be passed without unanimity. Roughly two-thirds of the votes are required to adopt legislation, with about a third necessary to block it. The number of votes is distributed according to the population of the Member States, but favours the smaller States.

Each EU enlargement has brought about an extension of QMV and a reduction in the use of the national veto. This erosion of national sovereignty and the consequential loss of the national veto has been one of the most controversial issues for British Governments.

Note that we are now referred to as a member state, and that our national voice has diminished to one of the many of the 'united states of Europe' that can be out-voted at every turn. Member States need to find allies with sufficient voting strength in order to form a blocking minority and prevent the adoption of an act.

A Single Market. One of the main aims of the SEA was to create a Single Market within the European Community by 1992; the objective being, to remove barriers and to increase harmonisation and competitiveness among its countries.

A common market is a first stage towards a single market, a type of trading bloc which is composed of a free trade area to facilitate the free movement of capital, labour, goods, and services between the members. The EEC was the first example of a both common and single market, but it was an economic union as it combined a customs union.

In October 1990, John Major and Foreign Secretary, Douglas Hurd, finally persuaded Mrs Thatcher to allow Britain to join the Exchange Rate Mechanism (ERM). The plan was that it would reduce exchange rate variability and achieve monetary stability in Europe, would prepare us for Economic and Monetary Union and finally, the introduction of a single currency (euro).

Billions of pounds were spent, in a useless attempt to defend the currency's value, after the pound sterling came under alarming pressure from currency speculators. The ensuing crash of the 16th September 1992 was subsequently labelled "Black Wednesday".

Britain's exit from the ERM caused the Conservative Party opinion poll ratings to plummet, never to fully recover, and although the economy began to show signs of recovery, after departure from the ERM, the recession wasn't declared over until the end of 1993.

Whilst many people recall 'Black Wednesday' as a national disaster, some conservatives claim that the forced expulsion from the ERM was a "Golden Wednesday" which paved the way for an economic revival.

*

The recession of the early 1990's was beginning to affect my work forcing me onto the dole queue but I didn't mind too much because it was a glorious summer, of which I spent much cultivating my garden, planting a few trees, building a 'cold-frame' (a wooden conservatory), and taking a well earned rest while circumstances permitted. I must have had one of the best kept gardens in the town centre, and great neighbours. Happy days!

My trees are coming along nicely as was the lawn, and the flowerbeds are award-winning. I think I'll lie on top of the garden wall (it's only 5feet high) and soak up the afternoon sun, while sending up the Zzz's. Then when Janet comes home from work; we'll drink and chat over the wall, during the course of the warm summer evening, and share the pleasanter pursuits in life, of good company and friendship. Pure heaven!

I had resigned myself to the back seat of current affairs during my term of unemployment, as most of what was happening was out of my (a mere tradesman's) control, there was no democracy anymore, as far as I could see.

The country was in a mess, and moreover, total European integration was inevitable after all this time of gutless subservience by our 'quisling' establishment. The insidious creep of EU domination was relentless. The Maastricht Treaty was signed on the 7th February 1992 by the members of the European Community, creating the European Union, making us

EU citizens, including the Queen, handing over huge swathes of power and influence to the unelected institutions of the EU.

The Maastricht Treaty didn't come into force until the following year on the 1st November 1993.

John Major had promised to keep Britain at the heart of Europe, and claimed to have won "game, set and match for Britain" by negotiating the social chapter and single currency opt-outs from the Maastricht Treaty, and by ensuring that there was no overt mention of a Federal Europe. Even so, several Conservative MPs, known as the Maastricht Rebels, voted against the treaty, causing irreparable damage to Major's authority in parliament.

*

I was managing quite well, and life was sweet under the circumstances. Oh didn't I mention a business partnership in 1991 which subsidised by me made a complete loss, that as well as gobbling up my life savings, put me into debt to the tune of £50k in less than 12 months. I was unemployed, penniless, although I did manage to hold onto my house, which was much better than most people faired at that time, with mortgage interest rates at 15%, and repossessions at a record high, and pretty hacked-off. So please excuse me if I appear to be slightly unconcerned or a little indifferent; I had become 'world weary', but ho-hum, a lesson learned, and the back garden beckoned. Now! Where's the sun cream?

My guardian angels must have been close by, because far from being miserable and becoming withdrawn, through staring into the face of adversity, there came, great pleasure, happiness and opportunity. I was able, with the extraordinary, kind and professional help and advice, from my accountant Mr Morrison FCA, to dispose of my residual stock and pay off a good portion of my debt.

Now was the time to batten down the hatches and weather the storm. The recession ended in1993, my work picked up and business flourished in the most amazing way, helping me to pay off the rest of my debt week by week, month by month, and year by year. I was back on my feet again!

During this interlude I met Claire. I'd been called out to do some electrical repairs to a house in Cox Green in Maidenhead. The girl who owned the house introduced me to her lodger who was extremely attractive, a lot younger than me and managed the local newsagents. She sat on the settee and we spoke while I was up the steps fixing the centre light. I then worked behind the settee fixing the 13amp socket on the wall where she leaned over the sofa to watch me work. Anyway I continued working for about another 40 minutes and she began to help; I then finished, got paid and left, remaining completely professional the whole time. Around teatime that evening the phone rang, asked for the electrician and said: "you called to my house today; do you remember"? I did. "You have an admirer; can you guess who it is?" Now this girl was married with two children but I suspected it was her, so I had to put her off without being nasty, so I said "oh! is it Claire?" not really thinking that it was. To which she replied "yes it is; I'll go and get her". We arranged a date and went out together, and got on really well. I'd help her open up at 5.30am in the morning and help deliver the newspapers if one of her 'paper-boys' didn't turn up. I was one of the best paid paper-boys in Berkshire, got a cooked breakfast and very generous perks. I didn't intend this to be a permanent relationship though and thought it would fizzle out in a few weeks but I wasn't in a strong position, what with being in debt and virtually unemployed, so I decided to maintain the status quo a little longer; after all she was very pretty, kind and attentive to my needs and we were happy together. Despite this pleasant relationship I knew that it wasn't to be a permanent one, but Claire was determined and my beautiful son was born the following year on the 8th November 1994.

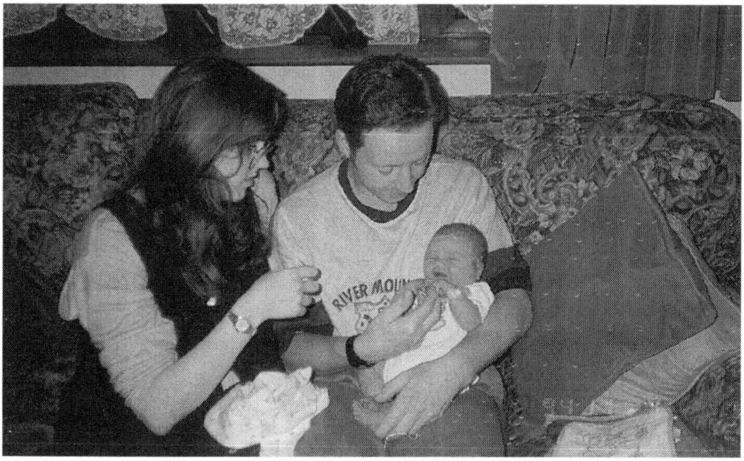

Claire and me with our new born son

My plan had always been to clear my debt, work hard, save enough money and then go to train in Japan; study the language and culture and live there. But family life beckoned, putting a huge strain on me. I had barely escaped one disastrous escapade and needed to get away. That failed business adventure had the direst effect on me and marked a turning point in my life. I was ready to give up on England and start a new life somewhere else but the lord moves in mysterious ways.

Although I had became engrossed in my work, in the most delightful way, doing the job that I loved and was cut out for, until I had saved enough money to fulfil a lifetime ambition: to live and train in Japan as 'uchi-deshi'. I realised that dream in June 1997, setting off to start my 6 month stay at 'Hoitsugan' dojo in Tokyo; this was the home of Nakayama Sensei, head of the Japan Karate Association (JKA).

To say that it was a culture shock would be an understatement! I was okay until I left 'Narita International Airport' where everyone was bilingual, and the signage was international (in English), but as I stepped off the airport express onto the platform at Ueno station, I was horrified to find myself surrounded by hordes of Orientals, all with the same, dark coloured hair, and everything written in 'Kanji' (pictograms) strange that, isn't it? Not what you'd expect to find in the middle of Tokyo.

Sitting on my bags, with my face in my hands I didn't move for an age, probably about an hour. As I sat there, I realised that everyday life just continued to happen all around me, and would continue to do so with or without me. It was up to me to participate and engage. Then with my limited knowledge of the Japanese language, I walked over to the ticket office and enquired: *Sumimasen ga, Ebisu made kippu o kaimasu ka? Domo. Nan sen to nan ji desu ka? Ah so desu ka, domo arigato gozaimashita.* Basically, what I said was: 'Could I buy a ticket to Ebis, what platform is it and what time does it leave? Thank you very much'.

As I waited for my train, feeling quite pleased with myself for successfully negotiating the first hurdle, I began to notice, that below all the signs and notices written in Japanese, was an English translation. Feeling more confident after the initial panic attack, I continued my journey, experimenting with my Japanese language as I went. Arriving at Ebis, I needed the toilet, so dashed over to the nearby public convenience, found an empty cubicle, locked the door behind me and that crucial moment; a hole in the ground! No toilet paper! I now know why those pretty young girls in the street, were handing out free miniature packets of tissues, heavily adorned with advertising. Doh!

Finally I arrived at JKA Headquarters which wasn't far from the station, (the Japanese railway system is second to none). Come to think of it I didn't drive a car, read an English newspaper or watch an English program for my entire stay in Japan. Once registered, I was taken around the corner to the Hoitsugan, and introduced to four others who were also *uchi-deshi* (live-in students). I was then shown around and given a room by a young lad named Offer, from Israel, who spoke good English, and with whom I became best friends. The others were: Hammed from Saudi Arabia, Zoubir, an Algerian French citizen and Magino, a Brazilian with a Japanese father.

The Hoitsugan was for foreign visitors, which gave them a place to stay in Japan, and train cheaply, 35,000 yen/month (san man go sen en). In 1997, that was about £75 a week. There were other day visitors, like Dan and Kevin from California, that had lived and worked in Japan for over ten years, who had initially come as 'uchi-deshi' but stayed on, and had remained Hoitsugan members. Our resident teacher was Kawawada Sensei; a high ranking (7th Dan) JKA Instructor, and our *Senpai* (senior), Kawawada Sensei's assistant and interpreter, called Leon from Iran, who had also been in Japan a long time, and spoke fluent Japanese. It was his job to make sure that we were comfortable and happy, ate proper food (meat) and didn't drink too much. In fact, he felt responsible for us, referring to us as his brothers, and family.

Holtsugan - Nakayama's private dojo - Ebis, Tokyo
Back Row: Magino - Offer - Dan
Front row: Leon senpai (our senior)
Zoubir - Kawawada sensei (Teacher) - Me

Incidently, something worth mentioning is that JKA instructors are full time professionals. They are the elite, recruited from the best Japanese university clubs. The JKA instructor programme aims to produce world class practioners; and they do. They ooze inner confidence and power, and possess an innate fighting spirit (*Samurai*) that puts them head and shoulders above the rest.

As Hoitsugan residents, we were required to train three mornings a week from 7 till 8.30am, then the rest of the day was our free time. During the day I attended language school until 4.30pm and trained again at JKA Honbu Dojo (JKA main dojo) from 6 till 8pm every evening. The experience at each dojo was completely different. At the Hoitsugan, we all felt a sense of loyalty and commitment, after all, Kawawada Sensei was given the privilege to teach in chief instructor, Master Nakayama's (head of JKA) own private dojo for the benefit of us, his overseas students (*gaijin*), and was there every morning at 6.45am waiting for us to get out of bed. Before and after each session, the most junior student would fetch a bucket of warm water, and we would then all take a floor cloth, in line, in unison, and wash the floor from end to end. It was a very simple and effective process really; in a line, place the cloth on the floor in front of you; bend and place your hands on the cloth, and push. The entire floor was cleaned in two or three minutes; simple!

As you can imagine, its effect were many fold. Teamwork, discipline and a pre warm up; and respect for your seniors and workplace. The main dojo, although still adhering to the same strict discipline, had many more students and operated as a commercial but non profit making organisation. Please don't be put off by my narrative of events, because even though I was chastised almost every day for one thing or another, it's not their fault.

The Japanese people are very kind, friendly and extremely hospitable, and they know how to behave, moreover, it's the safest country in the world. They're just a little bemused and slightly irritated when we fail to conform to, what comes perfectly natural to them, that which is normal, everyday Japanese life. Confused? I was. I'll give you a clue, for example: whistling, forgetting to bow after making eye contact with Sensei, and don't ever forget to take your shoes off inside (change to a different pair when entering the lavatory), okay. Oh! and something useful to learn before entering is to knock three times; if engaged, you will hear a polite reciprocal signal from the other side. Rather quaint don't you think?

If in the dojo, and you are the senior grade, you take the warm-up, unless there is a Japanese in the class. It doesn't matter that he is your junior in rank or age, he's JAPANESE. Furthermore, you never speak English in the dojo unless asked to translate to non Japanese, as I had to do once to a full class of Germans, who had just arrived for two weeks training. There was the instructor giving commands in Japanese to Germans, who listened to them, through me, in English; clever, eh? Not unusual though. I found that all foreigners spoke to each other in English; after all, it is the preferred language of international communication.

After an evening training session, we were always invited out to a restaurant, a bar or to someone's house for a party (a meal and a drink), the company was always mixed, and the girls were stunning. Through the language school, I was introduced to a group of Japanese friends, and became part of that group. In Japanese life, these groups usually meet at kindergarten and remain friends throughout their life. It was here that I met and fell in love with Kayoko (ko is the suffix for the female gender). My Senpai told me, that the best way to immerse yourself into Japanese language and culture, is to have a Japanese girlfriend (*koibito*). I did, and it changed my life overnight.

If you stay in Japan long enough, you begin to doubt your own native way of life. It happened to me, in this way: did grown men drink tea with milk and sugar, from a cup with a little handle on the side? Did we really mix milk and sugar with white rice? And did we ever wash ourselves in our own dirty bathwater? Of course you know, or then again you may not, that the Japanese wash outside the bathtub before getting in. You forget how to tie your shoelaces; you find yourself bowing to everybody you meet, even in the street, in broad daylight; also during a telephone conversation. You squat while waiting for a bus; it's really true! I did it, but convinced myself that it was part of my flexibility training. Furthermore, you never cross the road, until you hear that little tune, and are indicated to do so, even if there isn't a car in sight. It's a strange and very wonderful country, where you carry your 'alien' card, and sometimes feel like one too.

When I returned home to England, it took me two weeks to adjust. It was the most amazing feeling; I was walking around with a permanent smile on my face, watching people shopping and talking. Talking English! They appeared to me, to be speaking and chewing gum at the same time, you know, mouths opening and closing on every utterance. If you observe a Japanese in conversation, you'll notice that they draw their words back and don't move their lips as much, often finishing in; oh! Or is that just me? Anyway, after a few months of settling in and once back into my old routine, I really began to miss Japan, the climate, my friends and the most agreeable social life. As time went on, my adventure became more and more distant and detached from reality. Was it all a dream?

My first port of call on returning home was to my sister June. She had looked after my affairs whilst I was away; my house, my work-van and my son. It was good to be back! My son was there as I walked in; he looked lost and sad, staring at me as he slowly walked toward me, dropping his toy and stretching out his arms to be picked up. It was all in slow motion, as if he wasn't sure, but deep down he knew me. What had I done?

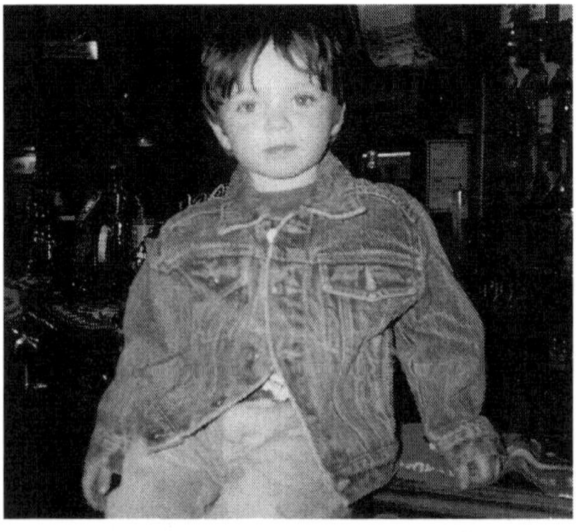

My son aged 2 and a half

I'd left this little boy for what must have seemed like an age, to him; when I left he could only speak baby talk, now we were having a full conversation. It was amazing! He held on tight then, after a while, fell asleep in my arms. How selfish was I? I felt awful and guilty and swore to myself that I would never leave him ever again; and I never have. Next, I phoned his mother, who wanted to see me immediately. She sounded upset and confused.

We met in the Queens head in Maidenhead and I realised that there would be no going back. She sobbed bitterly and chastised me for not staying in contact with her; she loved me; we had a son. It wasn't her fault that she had found someone else and was now engaged to be married. Well, that was it! I arranged to see my son on the weekend and continued with that arrangement for the next nine years.

My son and his mother

Then one evening my son phoned to tell me he had run away. He had told me that he was not happy at home: 'mummy's never at home; I rarely see her. He (stepfather) looks after us and takes us to school; I have his surname and even have to call him dad. I'm going to run away' WHOA! Listen son, I need to know where you are at all times. If things get too bad, call me; and if you have to leave the house, go to a friend nearby, okay! The school were concerned that my son wouldn't respond to his name saying: 'that's not me, I'm Joe Wight'.

Anyway, back to the phone call. 'Joe! Where are you?' 'It's okay Dad, I did what you said; I'm at my friends house'. 'Where is it, what's the address?' 'It's next door'. 'Stay there, I'm coming over'. When I arrived I talked to the parents and the police are called. They tell me to take him back with me to my house and they'll send an officer as soon as possible. Two officers turn up a couple of hours later and ask my son lots of questions. They then turn to me asking if I have a legal document confirming parental responsibility. I have, and show it to them. They tell me that my son is confident and happy and wants to live here with me. 'Do you want him?' 'Yes of course I do' I reply, 'but the courts will never allow it' I say. 'We are the Law and are convinced that this is where your son wants to be; leave the courts to us. Goodnight and take care of your son'. Just like that! I now look after him as a single parent. Things never worked out quite as I'd planned; it seems that I wasn't to be a family man, in the traditional sense that my brother and sisters are, but I remain optimistic, resigning myself to the fact that there's always something just around the corner!

My sister told me how the nation was grieving at the sad loss of Diana, princess of Wales, and how it had brought the country to a standstill; combined, with the transfer of sovereignty over Hong Kong, from the United Kingdom, to the People's Republic of China, and the landslide election for New Labour, 1997 had been a momentous year. Had it not?

*

In the run-up to the 2004 European elections I received a leaflet from the UK Independence Party through the letter box notifying residents of a local public meeting. I attended, was impressed with what I had heard, and joined UKIP there and then.

I remember thinking that I'd been waiting for this party all my adult life, because of its no-nonsense common sense policies. I became actively involved delivering thousands of leaflets, erecting dozens of UKIP display boards and attending all the public meetings, and would like to think that I contributed in a small way in helping UKIP achieve its first major electoral victory, coming third and winning 12 MEPs.

Within the sphere of the Mighty EU, UKIP were an irrelevance to be swatted away like 'gadflies, cranks and fruitcakes' or 'closet racist, and loonies' and, wait for it; 'BNP in blazers'. We've had it all! As Mahatma

Gandhi said;

"First they ignore you,
then they ridicule you,
then they fight you,
then you win."

We have reached the fourth stage.

The EU was not going to let the protestations of a mere democracy stand in their way, to total domination of Europe behind closed doors were they? Then on the 1st May 2004 they pressed ahead with the largest single expansion of the EU, both in terms of territory, number of states and population, however not in terms of gross domestic product (wealth).

The simultaneous accessions concerned the following countries: Cyprus, Czech Republic, Estonia, Hungary, Latvia, Lithuania, Malta, Poland, Slovakia and Slovenia. Seven of these were members of the former Soviet bloc, with one from the former Yugoslavia and the remaining two being Mediterranean islands.

Part of the same wave of enlargement was the accession of Bulgaria and Romania in 2007, which were unable to join in 2004 but, constitute, according to the Commission, part of the fifth enlargement. As of May 2011, there are no longer any special restrictions on the free movement of citizens of these new member states.

*

As the casualties of the Iraq war in 2004 mounted, Blair was accused of misleading Parliament, and his popularity dropped dramatically. That combined with the Blair-Brown pact, and low approval ratings, together with the reduction of their overall majority in the 2005 general election put mounting pressure on him to resign.

Blair announced publicly that he would step down as party leader, and at a special party conference in Manchester on the 24th June 2007, he formally handed over the leadership of the Labour Party to Gordon Brown. One of Blair's final traitorous acts before leaving office was to sign the Lisbon Treaty without the promised referendum, probably, as speculated by media, in the hope of becoming the first President of the European Council.

Gordon Brown assumed office the same afternoon as Blair's departure on the 27th June 2007; he had been the longest-serving (1997 to 2007) Chancellor of the Exchequer in modern history, and the longest prime minister in waiting.

Just in case anyone ever tries to tell you that, for all his faults, Gordon Brown was an economic genius, it is worth pointing out that the price of gold reached around £1,000 per ounce by November 2011. Yet between 1999-2002 he sold 395 tons (60%) of this nation's reserves for less than £200 per ounce.

That's a loss of over £10 billion and counting. If that was not a crime enough, he also announced to the markets the 17 separate auctions, how much he was going to sell, and on what date; leaving our public finances in the most disastrous state. What did Brown invest much of the proceeds of that poor sale in? The Euro of course! It has already been called 'the worst economic judgment ever made by a Chancellor' I suspect one day history will be even more brutal.

When Tony Blair was prime minister he handed over more power to Brussels bureaucrats in 2001 when he signed the Treaty of Nice that came into force in 2003, which prepared the EU for its 2004 enlargement and paved the way for the Treaty of Lisbon.

In October 2004, a proposed constitutional treaty was signed by all but two representatives from EU member states. The rejection by France and Holland consequently, effectively killed it off. After a "period of reflection" the EU leaders decided to write a new treaty to include most of the provisions of the original, and rename it the 'Reform Treaty' later to be known as the Lisbon Treaty.

This rebranded version of the EU constitution would be a major step towards a European Super-state, which will eventually wipe out individual nations. Unelected 'who are you?' Herman Van Rom...whatsisname would become its president, and the equally unheard of foreign policy lightweight, Cathy Ashton, its High Representative.

All that was needed was for the 27 nations to ratify the treaty for it to come into force; which all did, except Ireland, who were ordered to go and vote again, and told not to come back until they had the correct answer. How's that for local democracy?

In UKIP, I had found what I was looking for; I could take an interest in politics again and vote for a party that I truly believed in. After joining the party I became completely active, attending conferences and meetings, reading up on all the policies, leafleting and canvassing. Then I stood in my first Parliamentary election in 2005, and afterwards in local elections where I received my best result; coming second to the conservative incumbent, beating labour into 3rd place. Off the back of this great result, I was asked by the Maidenhead branch to join them, and was immediately selected to be their Parliamentary Candidate.

They were a well established group and we got straight on to preparing for the next general election that could come at any time. I wrote to the local paper and managed to get my letters published about once a month, on average, and in addition to that, a small group of us would go into the High Street every Friday morning campaigning and collecting signatures for the 'Better off Out' petition to leave the EU. The response was very encouraging with almost 8 out of 10 signing.

Myself and Nigel Farage MEP

Stuart Wheeler, who once donated £5 million to the Conservative Party, their biggest donation ever; after criticising David Cameron's stance towards the Lisbon Treaty and the European Union, donated £100,000 to UKIP on the 28th March 2009. He later joined, and was appointed treasurer in 2011 to spearhead fundraising in advance of the 2014 European elections. This was a shot in the arm for UKIP, because of Wheeler's network of contacts. Party leader Nigel Farage said the move would enable the party to raise serious money, as a lack of funds was holding us back.

The Right Honourable Norman Tebbit MP is often misquoted as saying directly to the unemployed "get on your bike and look for work" actually said: 'I grew up in the 1930's with an unemployed father. He didn't riot. He got on his bike and looked for work, and he kept looking 'til he found it'. After Major came back from Maastricht with an opt-out from the Social Chapter and the single currency, Tebbit was one of the few MPs to criticise the new powers the Community would acquire in the debate on the 18th December 1991.

He claimed the government had been on the defensive against "federalist follies" and that Maastricht had seen "a series of bridgeheads into our constitution, into the powers of this House, and into the lives of individuals and businesses". He decided not to stand in the 1992 election, in order to devote more time caring for his wife, who was permanently disabled in the IRA's bombing of the Grand Hotel in Brighton, and after the election was granted a life peerage and entered the House of Lords, resuming his fight against the Maastricht Treaty.

At the October 1992 Conservative Party Conference in Brighton, Tebbit embarrassed John Major's government when he made a speech attacking the Maastricht Treaty. As he walked up onto the podium he was applauded whilst holding aloft a copy of the Treaty. He asked the conference a series of questions about it, saying: did they want to see a single currency or be citizens of a European Union? The audience shouted back "No!" after each question, after which he received a tumultuous standing ovation as he walked into the centre of the Conference hall waving amongst the cheers of 'Norman the conqueror'.

In March 2007 he became patron of the cross-party 'Better Off Out' campaign which advocates British withdrawal from the EU. In a statement explaining his support he said: "From being a supporter of British membership of the Common Market in 1970 I have come to believe that the United Kingdom would be Better Off Out of the developing European Republic of the 21st century. We British have a thousand year history of self-government. We have been free and democratic longer than any other nation.

The European Union is too diverse, too bureaucratic, too corporatist and too centralist to be a functioning democracy. We are happy to trade with our European friends and the rest of the world – but we would prefer to govern ourselves". In March 2009 Norman Tebbit revealed that he would vote for UKIP, urging voters to snub the main three political parties in the upcoming EU Parliament election, suggesting they use the European election to send a message to the implicated parties. He pointed out that there were a series of smaller parties people could vote for in addition to UKIP, including the Green Party, but he urged against voting British National Party.

All the signs were looking good for UKIP to do well in the forthcoming 2009 European elections. In the print and broadcast media 'UKIP' was the 'buzz' word; we were also gaining support on the doorstep, as well as collecting thousands of signatures for the 'Better Off Out' petition. UKIP public meetings were in abundance, with standing room only, and the weather was glorious.

If Cameron hadn't made that broadcast two days before the election, reminding us, that all the major parties had promised a referendum in the 2005 Election; that the Lisbon treaty (EU constitution) includes a massive transfer of powers from the nation states of Europe to Brussels, and that the best way to get that referendum is to vote conservative this Thursday 4th June 2009, UKIP would have done much better, or probably won.

Notable outcomes as shown below, was the significant drop in support for the Labour Party, in its 12th year in government, who came third, and UKIP finishing second in a major election for the first time in its history.

	David Cameron Conservative	Nigel Farage UKIP	Gordon Brown Labour
Last election	27 seats	12 seats	19 seats
Seats won	26	13	13
Seat change	- 1	+1	- 6
Popular vote	4,198,394	2,498,226	2,381,760
Percentage	27.7%	16.5%	15.7%

UKIP received the second highest share of the vote, defeating Labour and the LibDems.

We in Maidenhead began making plans for the 2010 General Election immediately, increasing our leafleting and distribution of DVD's, letters to the Press and canvassing. We secured an Election Office in the Town Centre, kindly donated by one of our members; all with the aim of raising our profile and getting our message out to maximise our vote share.

On the 6th April, Gordon Brown went to Buckingham Palace to ask the Queen to dissolve Parliament, and call new elections, which took place the following month on the 6th May. UKIP contested 572 of the 649 seats across the UK, with its main target being the Buckingham seat of the Speaker John Bercow, which Nigel had stepped down as leader in November 2009, to concentrate on.

In the run up to the election, Jenny Sleep, the mainstay of our branch became terminally ill with cancer; it came as a terrific blow and wounded me deeply. Of course I wanted to continue and do well, but without Jenny, who was a human dynamo, and had worked so hard, I felt depleted. I was on the ropes. Then ominously, on the morning of polling day, Nigel took that fateful decision to climb aboard a light aircraft in a publicity stunt that went wrong. The aeroplane crashed while trying to scoop up a trailing banner, which got caught up in its tail plane causing the aircraft to nosedive into the airfield.

Watching the newsreels of the wreck in stunned silence, it seemed impossible that anyone could survive. There was Nigel trapped by his harness, thankfully; hanging upside down in his seat with his head in the mud. Subsequent photo's, by the grace of God, showed Nigel being pulled from that wreckage and miraculously being led away, albeit, bloodied and bruised, and in a dreadful state.

Both Nigel and the pilot survived with non-life-threatening injuries. He admitted afterwards though, that it had been a silly thing to do, as he has a fear of flying, adding that the ordeal had left him weak and shaken. With my expectations previously raised on the strength of our amazing European Election results, I was now beginning to sink, things were happening that were out of our control. This wasn't going to be the time we make our breakthrough, we'd be lucky to get our deposit back, which is 5% of the vote.

The count didn't get under way until 2am, I was feeling despondent, and after a 3 hour wait decided to call it a day and get to bed. Theresa May Conservative MP for Maidenhead saw her share of the vote increase by a massive 7.6% to 59.5% totalling just under 32,000 votes. Although the overall national Tory vote went up, with a seat change of plus 97, they were 20 seats short of an overall majority, resulting in a hung parliament where no party was able to command a majority in the House of Commons.

UKIP polled 3.1% of the vote (919,471 votes), but took no seats. This made it the party with the largest percentage of the popular vote to win no seats in the election (In a fully proportional system, 3.1% of 649 seats would be just over 20 seats). David Cameron's 'cast iron' guarantee on a referendum, which he later reneged upon probably, prevented a large part of the Tory Eurosceptic wing from swinging to UKIP.

Following the failure of negotiations between the Labour Party and the Liberal Democrats to form a coalition government, Brown tendered his resignation as Prime Minister to the Queen and recommend that she invite the Leader of the Opposition, David Cameron, to form a government. Coalition talks began immediately between the Conservatives and the Liberal Democrats. David Cameron formed a government in the Queen's name and became Prime Minister, ending 13 years of a Labour government.

It was back to the drawing board for UKIP. Lord Pearson resigned as leader in August 2010, and Nigel Farage was re-elected against Professor Tim Congdon, David Campbell Bannerman and Winston McKenzie with more than 60% of the vote. During his acceptance speech, he spoke out against the Coalition government, saying that the Conservative Party's policy on Europe can be summed up as: "Surrender, surrender, surrender".

Throughout my term at the Maidenhead branch I was very keen to have some sort of local UKIP newspaper, but the cost and distribution would always hold us back. Then I discovered that I could write a good letter, and consequently, get it published on a regular basis in the local paper. The *Maidenhead Advertiser* held an exclusive 20,000 readership, distributed and paid for. Brilliant!

The problem we had nationwide though, was that the coverage of UKIP's activities in the mainstream media was comparatively small; that was until the *Daily Express* launched its crusade on the 8th January 2011 in the form of a 'Special Edition' entitled *GET BRITAIN OUT OF THE EU*. We demand our country back! Every day since, they have reported on how our continued membership of the EU is destroying our country, and affecting every aspect of our daily lives. We couldn't have hoped to reach that amount of people with our own publication. It was a God-send! Furthermore, many of the other newspapers have jumped on the 'bandwagon' since, giving us much needed exposure. All this additional coverage has definitely given us a boost and helped to increase our membership, not to mention the almost weekly defections.

In the local elections on the 6th May 2011, UKIP won nine out of the seventeen seats for Ramsey Town Council, and on the 12th May, UKIP councillor Lisa Duffy was elected as Mayor. *The Daily Mail* claimed that UKIP "has made political history after taking control of its first council in the UK". The defections to UKIP have continued, with amongst the most recent, high profile being, Lord Hesketh 10th October 2011, and Roger Helmer at the UKIP Spring Conference 2012.

At the Maidenhead branch UKIP AGM in February 2012, I announced my resignation as PPC and branch committee member with the idea of taking a back seat for a while. I really needed a rest, but it was to be short lived. As I sat in my living room gazing out across the golf course, it suddenly dawned on me that Slough was just the other side of those trees and didn't have a functioning UKIP branch; in fact it had been dormant for some while. No! I told myself, I need a rest, and quickly put the idea out of my head.

Each day for the next two three days, the thought kept creeping back, stronger and stronger each time until finally I woke up to the possibility of re-starting the Slough Branch. I made some enquiries, did some research then contacted the UKIP South East office to tell them that I was interested in re-forming the branch in Slough. A meeting was arranged to take place at the 'Centre', 150 letters were sent out to members and inquirers and the hall was full. I introduced myself, saying that 'as a long standing active UKIP member, former Windsor branch chairman, and parliamentary candidate for Maidenhead for the last 5 years, I was delighted to take over the Slough branch, just recently, when the opportunity arose to do so'.

Being Slough born and bred, it was always my first choice so I didn't hesitate. Officers were elected; I was selected as Branch Chairman and also as PPC (Prospective Parliamentary Candidate) and the branch was duly formed. It was all very exciting, and we had got off to a good start. We were immediately thrown into local elections, fielding a full set of 14 candidates, contesting every ward. The response during the three week campaign was tremendous. The local newspapers were very interested in us and gave us lots of positive coverage, and although we didn't win any seats, we did double the amount of votes polled in the 2010 general election in Slough. '

We were on the up, I told the Press. 'In the short time since its re-formation, the branch has been totally committed and active, and is already planning for the next local election (2014), where the full council of 42 seats are up for re-election, and as before, we intend to field a full slate of candidates'.

*

Often, people say that we shouldn't keep looking back into the past. We can't change anything, and it'll never be how it was fifty or sixty years ago. Well, I'm not suggesting that we can turn the clock back, that would be a ridiculous assumption, but that we are what we are, because of where we have come from, can learn from our mistakes and begin to put things right. We've lost our way, and now it's a matter of resetting our course and realigning ourselves.

Mass immigration, the dogma of multiculturalism and the growing power of the European Union have conspired to undermine our British nationhood. I have seen my own town change beyond recognition to such an extent that I feel like a foreigner in my own country. Our once unified country is in danger of becoming nothing more than a land mass filled with disparate peoples.

Whole streets, estates, and in fact a good portion of Slough's indigenous population has been replaced by migrants from all over the world. Most of my friends, neighbours and the people I grew up with, gave up and moved away long ago. They felt helpless, and complained that a vote for any party was a waste of time, and that for many years; any talk of immigration was taboo.

The left pushed ahead with its ill-conceived social engineering experiment as the PC brigade rode shotgun to make sure anyone who dared protest about the flood of immigrants was immediately branded a racist. Travel around our big cities and you'll be excused for thinking you're in a foreign land. That's not prejudice it's a fact borne out by the official figures. Go to Slough, Blackburn or Birmingham and you discover thousands of children growing up in homes where they are the only family members with much grasp of English.

Shop in Harrow, north-west London, on a Saturday afternoon and you can go several minutes at a time without hearing a single English voice. Drive through some inner-city suburbs of our capital and you can be excused for thinking you're in Kabul or Karachi. I'm sure David Cameron doesn't want to be remembered as the PM whose election slogan was: we will make sure every child in Britain grows up knowing a second language; preferably English.

How Slough has changed

In the 1960's I began to notice the exodus in Slough (white flight), as a result of the constant flow of immigrants into the UK that mostly came for work, systematically replacing the indigenous population. Southall, for example, was cleared in the 1950's, supposedly for redevelopment, and its inhabitants were resettled into new towns like Bracknell. So why was Southall then, afterwards, colonised by Asians?

The same thing happened in Slough but in a different way, and over a longer period. A whole new council housing estate was built in and around the village of Chalvey on what was previously green fields, and common land, then all the council tenants from the 1930's Manor Park estate were invited to move into these new open plan, pedestrianised, centrally heated modern houses, with their plastic taps and paper walls.

Incredibly, the offer was snapped up. Immigrants then settled into the old Manor park houses, so changing the whole make up of the community with their Mosques, shops, clothing and language.

Initiatives such as 'sons and daughters' schemes, which offered the children of council housing tenants priority based on a points system, and where references were needed to even get a look-in were abandoned, as they were deemed to be discriminatory.

The homeless became the priority and this idea of housing based on need was open to all sorts of interpretation and abuse.

Previous housing policy with strict vetting procedures, which were once a defining feature, favoured long-standing locals waiting to be housed. Their council houses became permanent. They may have paid rent to the council, but they were their homes and gave them a reason to have an investment in them, their gardens, their neighbourhoods and their estates in which a third of the population lived.

The 'Tower-blocks' and new council housing schemes that were built to replace the slums, by the end of the 1970's, were becoming slums themselves, where sub-letting was not only rife, but also illegal. Once Maggie Thatcher announced the 'right to buy' your council house at heavily discounted prices they were snapped up leading to an acute shortage of homes to rent. The result of what I call bad housing policies has meant that the area that I grew up in is now totally over-run with immigrants.

Slough has changed so much since I was a kid. Gone is the sense of pride and belonging, and flying the flag. What happened to the National anthem that used to be played at the end of the night in the cinema; still played in the British Legion though?

When I was in the infant school, I remember the entire school being given a Union Jack on a stick and walked to the Farnham Road with all the teachers, where both sides of the street were lined with 100's of kids from all the schools in the area. The Queen was scheduled to pass by, and we were to wave and cheer; that was really exiting!

I believe that this lack of patriotism is due to the loss of sovereignty over the years, through the EU treaties that have systematically stripped away our Nationhood and that since the Lisbon Treaty we have merely become a member state of Europe. We are no longer the Queens Subjects because of this act, but European citizens, as is the Queen. Maybe this is why so many no longer bother to vote?

Among the educated elite some argue that a changed population would be for the better and inevitable in a globalised world. So long as there is integration, a more diverse population would be more creative, innovative, stimulating, open minded and tolerant.

This view, though, is not shared with the UK population as a whole, who have never been consulted by politicians over a policy that allowed millions of migrants to enter the UK between 1997 and 2010. It is believed that Labour encouraged mass-immigration in the belief that the immigrants would vote for them. This would enhance Labour's electoral chances.

When Rochdale grandmother Gillian Duffy raised concerns with Gordon Brown over immigration she was branded a 'bigot'. Whatever the view a person holds on immigration, nobody should try to prevent the subject being fully and maturely debated. When properly controlled, immigration can bring expertise and industry to the economy, and enrich everything from cuisine to music, culture and theatre.

Silencing any dissenting voices with cries of racism, is an insult to democracy. The failed doctrine of multiculturalism, encourages immigrant communities to live in social and cultural isolation, with little attempt to integrate into the host community.

*

In the years before I left Slough I noticed many new faces appearing in the town, and living directly behind the High Street, I'd see these new migrants passing by my front door at an alarmingly increasing level. Things turned worse when my old neighbours either died or moved out; previously established Asian migrants were buying up the beautiful Victorian Town houses, turning them into 'bedsits' and filling them to the hilt with the newcomers. How could the council allow this to happen? They weren't all Eastern European, but Black Africans also.

I became more and more concerned when our relatively quiet neighbourhood began to turn uncomfortably noisy. These newcomers were rowing in the street, cars were being vandalised; my own work van was broken into and robbed right outside the house; and beer-halls were springing up in the High Street where there once stood established traders. The new 24 hour licensing laws only added to the misery, with people screaming and shouting at each other in the dead of night, and Police helicopters flying above the rooftops, literally, just outside my window in the small hours of the morning. Heaven help us!

This change coincided with the new Labour government and their open-door immigration policy; according to official figures, between 1997-2010 up to 5.5million people born outside the UK arrived as long-term migrants, not including an estimated further 1million illegals. Tony Bair, later, defended Labour's controversial mass-immigration policy by claiming that Britain cannot succeed unless it opens its borders to more people from different backgrounds.

Blair said it was 'right' that the country was made up of mixed cultures and faiths. He claimed migrants had made Britain 'stronger' and said those calling for greater curbs on foreigners were wrong. He added that there would be problems at certain points, but that those problems are to be overcome. Perhaps he meant overcome by 'White Flight'. Possibly the rise in migrants was a politically motivated attempt to change the nation. For me sadly, it was time to join the 'exodus'.

I put my house on the market and moved to a more rural setting, north of Slough. I was only a few miles outside of town and continued to work in the same way but from a different location, but saw my working week reduced to just 3 days a week, which didn't concern me too much because I'd sized-down and no longer had a mortgage.

A few years ago the BBC's Panorama program, investigated claims of how Slough had been transformed by the latest wave of migrant workers who have moved here, starting their new lives in thousands of rented rooms. This presented a particular challenge to the council over government funding, because council tax is paid per property not per person, putting an enormous strain on local services.

The council say that as many as 18 adults have been known to share a small 3 bed roomed house. That is not paying its way, and the numbers are increasing. Richard Bilton reporting said: "I saw something in Slough's back gardens I'd never seen before". He called them 'Beds in Sheds' that come complete with satellite dishes, but none of them legal.

They can cost as much as £150 a week; not that anyone admits to renting them out. One of these occupants was approached, who spoke little English, but was able to confirm that this indeed was his home. Most of the migrants he met were paying other migrants; one of them a Polish labourer on his weekly trip to pay his Asian landlord, had the door closed in his face as soon as he spotted the camera.

Zdizislaw Szymczzak who came to Slough over 60 years ago said that "I don't care what system you have in place, with no control it's going to break down". A recent YouGov poll graphically revealed that an overwhelming majority of the public appears not to support rapid demographic change that is under way.

The colossal scale of mass immigration in recent years represents a savage betrayal of the British people by our governing elite. No one ever voted for Britain to be transformed from a cohesive nation into a fractured multicultural society. Yet such a revolution has been brought about by the ideological trashing of our national identity and the wilful collapse of our borders, with the influx of foreign arrivals now running at almost 600,000 a year, most from Africa and Asia.

What we are witnessing is the systematic destruction of a once proud country. As the pace of change accelerates Britain is fast becoming a place without any mutual sense of belonging or any shared heritage or even a common language. The very concept of our British national identity is sinking into irrelevancy. In large swathes of our cities, amid the burkas and babble of foreign tongues, too many indigenous Britons now feel like aliens in their own land.

The revolutionary impact of mass immigration has been reinforced by astonishing figures that show two thirds of all babies born in London have foreign parents. In just six of the 32 boroughs in the capital were British parents in the majority, while in Newham, part of the East End, an incredible 84.1% of births were to migrants, most from India, Pakistan or Poland. Across London's schools white pupils are now in the minority.

Nor is London alone in this trend. In the East Midlands city of Leicester, where just 44% of school pupils are white, it seems likely that the majority of the overall Asian-dominated population could be non-white in the very near future, making it the first urban conurbation in Britain to achieve that landmark. Given the huge levels of immigration and high migrant birth rate several other cities will quickly follow.

In January 2010 Birmingham Council announced that the Asian children outnumbered white pupils in the local primary schools and it is probable that the city will have a non-white majority before the end of the decade. The same is true of Oldham and Bradford. According to one study by Oxford University, white Britons will be in a minority across the whole of the United Kingdom by 2066. In modern history no country has ever gone through such rapid social upheaval without being conquered by an enemy power. If this kind of enforced revolution were taking place elsewhere, Left-wingers would be outraged.

Fulminating about the rights of the indigenous population they would portray the change as a colonialist takeover, but when Britain's own nationhood is under threat they celebrate because they are the architects of this change. In government from 1997 to 2010 Labour cynically used mass immigration as a vast tool of social engineering to restructure Britain. The impression sometimes given is that uncontrolled immigration has been an accident, supposedly the result of administrative incompetence.

This outlook was largely adopted over the fiasco at the UK Border Agency, which was castigated in an official report over its failure to maintain proper checks. Yet the truth is that the Border Agency failed so dramatically in its work because Labour politicians wanted it to. They loathed the idea of a tough approach to immigration. A free-for-all is precisely what they desired to refashion Britain. As Tony Blair's aide Andrew Neather famously admitted, Labour sought to 'rub the Right's nose in diversity'. That is why they eagerly allowed the immigration rate to rocket by relaxing controls and dishing out passports, work permits and student visas like confetti. If New Labour had really wished to crack down on immigration they could easily have done so. However, the integrity of our position was destroyed from within by people who were filled with loathing for the traditions of our country, obsessed with the dogma of racial diversity and eager to expand their inner city client vote.

Their revolution was implemented against the will of the people through repression, whereby open debate was stifled through hysterical accusations of racism and through remorseless propaganda about the benefits of immigration, especially supposed economic growth and the 'cultural enrichment of our communities'. We can now see how hollow all that propaganda was. Mass immigration has brought falling living standards as millions of working-class Britons have been thrown on the economic scrap heap. The burdens on our infrastructure have become intolerable, from the costs of welfare benefits for migrants to the pressure on schools and housing. Contrary to all the upbeat rhetoric about diversity, immigration has also brought social dislocation, urban crime and gangland violence.

Even Trevor Philips, head of the equality and Human Rights Commission, recently admitted that 'some districts are on their way to becoming fully fledged ghettoes'. Moreover, alien practices have been imported into our once well-ordered society, as mass voter fraud, sharia law or exploitation of vulnerable white teenage girls. It is tragic to see Britain's continuing decline. The only way the process can be halted is by a government tough enough to bring back real immigration controls.

It is no secret that mass uncontrolled immigration is the reason for the lack of housing. Our population is growing at a grotesquely alarming rate, in fact it is out of control, and furthermore, in the name of multicultural diversity our national identity is being obliterated, but still, the established parties will not cite immigration as the cause.

Under Tony Blair, Labour tried to make the case that immigration was good for the economy. It's true that if you have more people, you have a bigger economy, but there is no significant benefit to GDP per head for the actual resident population.

Britain has become one of the most overcrowded nations in the Western world, placing unrelenting pressure on our infrastructure. The roads are in gridlock almost all day now, and 'rush hour' has become 'rush around the clock'. Put that alongside the amount of people that you see walking about the streets in Slough during the day, and it begs the question 'where and how do they live, and where do they get their money from?' it is incredible!

Thanks to both the influx of 600,000 arrivals every year and the soaring birth rate among migrants, there is a shortage of housing, but the government just will not come out and say it. Instead they are pushing the controversial National Planning Policy Framework, which in reality means more urban sprawl.

There are many solutions if we are short of labour. We can raise wages and draw more people into work; we can change working methods and our products. Immigration is not necessarily the answer unless we fail to train our own. It is certainly not the answer when you have other aspects like a housing crisis.

The property developers must be having a ball. This planning free-for-all is to cope with the estimated 5million increase in the population that will require 2million new homes to be built by 2020, which will without doubt see the destruction of our countryside and the huge loss of green open spaces. This is not just mere conjecture; it has already happened here in Slough and, is still going on, across the country. Such an approach is madness. A quarter of all births in Britain are now to foreign parents, rising to an incredible two thirds in London.

Politicians like to claim that the massive influx of migrants has boosted our prosperity, but the truth is that it has been matched by recession, unemployment and falling living standards. While ruthless employers have enjoyed cheap-labour, the working class have seen their wages driven down, with millions thrown on the scrapheap while more than 80% of new jobs go to immigrants.

Apart from the economics, mass immigration has been a disaster for Britain in a host of other ways, from corruption at the ballot box to the growing incidence of bogus marriages, from gangland crime to the importation of witchcraft and Islamic honour killings. UKIP has a tough line on immigration, saying that: they will have a 5 year ban on settled immigration, triple the number of border agency staff and find and deport all illegals.

Death of Robin Gibb

On Monday 20th May 2012, I heard on the breakfast time news at 9am, that Bee Gee Robin Gibb had died. When something like this happens, it puts a whole new perspective on your life. The Bee Gees have been part of my youth and when listening to their great sound I am transported back to that happy time in an instant. Broadcaster Paul Gambaccini described Robin Gibb as "one of the major figures in the history of British music with an incredibly witty sense of humour, and was fun to be around. Everyone should be aware that the Bee Gees are second only to Lennon and McCartney as the most successful song writing unit in British popular music", he said.

The music of the 1960's had the greatest effect on my early years, and I still claim it was the best pop music decade ever, never to be repeated.

The Bee Gees arrived late on the 1960's music scene, at the time when the great pop 'heavyweights' the Beatles and the Stones were moving away from the limelight, when on Top of the Pops one Thursday night, there they were, with Robin singing lead vocals of 'Massachusetts' with his distinctively amazing, clear vibrato voice, in tight harmony with brothers Barry and Maurice, producing their unmistakable, instantly recognisable sound.

They'd had an earlier hit with 'New York Mining Disaster 1941' but the sound was not dissimilar to that of the 'Merseysound' and was mistaken for a Beatles song as it was issued to radio stations with a blank white label listing only the song title. Some DJs immediately assumed this was a new single by The Beatles and started playing the song in heavy rotation. This helped the song climb into the Top 20 in both the United Kingdom and the United States. Make no mistake, the Bee Gees had arrived, they were the new pop sensation. The new musical giants!

Robin was behind the campaign for a permanent memorial to be built for the 55,573 aircrew of Bomber command that lost their lives in raids over Germany during the 2nd world war. Speaking of the campaign on television in 2011 he mentioned that he had been ill himself, adding that he had been diagnosed with liver cancer, he said 'I am determined to beat this and fully intend to be at the Unveiling ceremony in June.

On the 13th February 2012, Robin joined British military trio 'The Soldiers' for the Coming Home charity concert at the London Palladium, in support of injured servicemen. It was his first public appearance for almost five months, and his final one.

Robin Gibb sadly dies at 62 (1949-2012)

The Bomber Command Association and its many members were deeply saddened to learn that Robin Gibb died last night. We send our love and best wishes to Dwina and all the family. Robin has been a magnificent champion of the Bomber Command Memorial Campaign and without his devoted support and commitment we would not be where we are today.

His legacy will be his music; but so too his determination during his illness and from our perspective, his work as President of the Heritage Foundation which brought the Memorial to life. Throughout his illness Robin remained in close touch with the Association and visited the Memorial site earlier this year. Nonetheless, it is a tragedy that Robin will not see the finished article.

Robin did his bit for all who served in Bomber Command and on the behalf of the veterans and the relatives of those who died in WWII, we would simply like to say, thank you.
Malcolm White, Chairman
Bomber Command Association

I don't mind admitting that the sad news upset me and changed my plans for the day, and so I resolved to write my tribute to Robin and the Brothers Gibb instead, whilst listening to their early songs. Paul Gambaccini said on the News that he had listened to 'I started a joke' adding that anyone hearing that song today would have trouble holding back a tear. Well I did listen to it, and he was right. When Robin became ill last year the whole nation prayed for him, he acknowledged them when in remission and thanked them publicly for their support and kindness saying, he pulled through with their help.

Till I finally died,
Which started the whole world living,
Oh, if I'd only seen,
That the joke was on me.

Robin, the day you were born, the whole world started living; the day you died, the whole world has started crying. And the joke was never on you.

*

The Queen's Diamond Jubliee in June 2012 was a momentous year for patriotism, giving us much to feel proud about.

In this, her Diamond Jubilee, celebrating her reign of 60 glorious years, we all thought that thanks to her, the monarchy remains a respected and viable institution, and infinitely more appealing than an elected politician as President.

The Jubilee had been a wonderful hammer blow to the dogma of the pro-EU, multicultural progressives who mistakenly think that nationhood and the monarchy are outdated concepts. The mood of patriotism has never been stronger, nor has any British sovereign been more secure on the throne than Queen Elizabeth is today.

Then came the Olympics the following month, held in London 27th July - 12th August.

What a success. We really are a great nation, when we put our minds to it.

*

As I have mentioned earlier, I joined UKIP in 2004, because like many others I had become disillusioned with the mainstream parties. I felt that we were not living in a democratic country, and no matter who you vote for, you get pretty much the same thing. In any case, how could your MP or your party represent you while they are being controlled and told what to do by the institutions in Brussels. In fact, over 70% of our laws are made there by the EU commission, which rather makes Parliament redundant, doesn't it? UKIP's stance is to repeal the 1972 European Act, leave the EU and sign a free trade agreement. In other words; be friends with our European neighbours; trade with them, by not be governed by them.

Nigel knows that we will soon win more parliamentary seats but in order to do that we must win more seats on the local councils up and down the country. There are no short cuts! It means a lot of footwork, leafleting and door-knocking. In addition, it needs many people to write letters to the local newspapers.

Nigel was becoming a serious threat to the establishment parties and to protest groups, and was massively in demand. He was attacked in Edinburgh, hit with placards and 'egged' (who are the 'fruitcakes' now?) so it was now also necessary for him to have security with him at all public meetings, which he hated.

UKIP is the fastest growing party in Britain today with thousands joining us every month. It appeals to people across the political spectrum, based on its no-nonsense policies, although they don't tend to be concentrated in one area, but throughout the UK as a whole, which makes it difficult for us to win a majority. Past election results have shown that we are becoming the official opposition to Labour, beating them in Rotherham – a Labour heartland – and coming second to them in South Shields, Tyneside. We are also doing well in other areas by coming a close second in the solid Libdem seat of Eastleigh, Hants. Because of these astounding results, Nigel was interested in focusing on the Labour vote in 2014. With this in mind, I requested that Nigel visit Slough, it being a Labour stronghold; he didn't say no, which surprised me, but said he would come with the proviso that I field a full slate of

42 candidates. I was faced with a daunting task. I appointed my membership secretary as campaign manager, who worked his socks off. By the close of nominations we had 34 confirmed candidates and we went to Nigel with that. We didn't have time to arrange a public meeting at such short notice, so Nigel agreed to do a 'walkabout' at the Britwell shops followed by media interviews at the 'Lynchpin' Pub. Well I can tell you, it went better than I could have dreamed. All the press, radio and TV were there, it went without a hitch and made the six o'clock news. Job done!

When I went into this election, I was hoping to win a seat, maybe two or possibly three. It really depended on the turnout, but on the day of the count we only won one seat. The local press hailed it as a great success and major breakthrough for UKIP in Slough, against all the odds. This meant that, if you vote for UKIP you get UKIP!

Although the European elections were on the same day Thursday 22nd May 2014, we had to wait till Sunday, until all the votes in Europe had been cast and the polling stations had closed, before we could start our count.

In the face of massive hostility and opposition from the political and media establishment, we won a decisive victory; taking 24 seats across the country. We gained our first MEP in the North East and also in Scotland, and in the South East region four were elected. UKIP's popularity was souring with its membership topping 40,000; probably helped along by Nick Clegg's enormous miscalculation, in thinking that he could boost his ratings by challenging Nigel Farage in two national television debates.

In the second BBC TV debate on "Britain's future in Europe", a YouGov poll gave Farage 68% and Clegg 27%, a big increase on the first debate the week before, broadcast on LBC radio and Sky News, which Farage won by 57% to 36%.

The result as demonstrated by the polls showed Clegg to be a clear loser and not only gave UKIP massive publicity, but also political momentum for the European elections on the 22nd May. Nigel later thanked Nick Clegg for giving him this amazing opportunity and joked that 'Clegg' was really UKIP's secret weapon.

The biggest losers, I feel though, were the Labour and the Conservative parties, who's Messrs Milliband and Cameron didn't have the courage to take part and stand up for Britain's place in Europe. Preferring to bury their heads in the sand, and pretend that UKIP and

Nigel Farage were an irrelevance, but in reality, they were enraged and frustrated with this upstart, fledgling party of 'closet racist', 'loonies' and 'fruitcakes'. Their derogatory and sly mocking comments though, do not help them one iota. Instead, each time they "pick on the smallest kid in the playground" our numbers swelled; the public punished them by crossing the floor, joining-up or giving us their vote.

*

This was to be the end but after reading that James Garner had died, I felt compelled to add the following.

James Garner (7th April 1928 – 19th July 2014)

James garner, in my opinion was one of those real, larger than life actors who were part of my childhood by means of TV and Film. I can't remember when it was that I first saw him, because he was the star in more than 50 films but it was probably in the TV western series 'Maverick'.

I would like to pay tribute here, to a popular and charming, and one of my favourites; a true Hollywood legend.

"It's so sad to read of your passing in this morning's newspaper. Goodbye Jim and thank you for being part of my life."

I feel prompted by this sad news to also mention another of my all-time favourite films: The Great Escape in which James Garner played Flt. Lt. Robert Hendley, the "Scrounger"

When 'The Great Escape' was first released in 1963, I went to see it at the Ambassador cinema on the Farnham Road in Slough. It told the true story of a mass break-out of captured airmen from a high-security German prisoner of war camp, Stalag Luft III, in 1943. This was only 18 years after the end of the 2nd world war, when many of those who survived were still alive.

The film opens, accompanied by the unforgettable soundtrack, with the prisoners (among them, the most hardened escapees) arriving on trucks at the newly built camp. This proved to be a monumental mistake by the Germans in that it provided 'Big X', RAF Squadron Leader Roger Bartlett with every 'escape artist' in Germany, who immediately set about plans for an ambitious escape attempt of 250 prisoners.

An escape committee was formed and it was decided that three tunnels would be started, codenamed Tom, Dick and Harry. 'Harry' went northerly from hut 104. 'Dick' went westerly from hut 122 and 'Tom' went parallel to 'Dick' from hut 123.

Bartlett: *If the goons find one, we'll move into the other.*

Teams were then organised to tunnel, make civilian clothing and forge documents, etc. Flight Lieutenant Robert Hendley, (James Garner) an American in the RAF, is the 'scrounger' whose job it is to find what is needed, i.e. clothes, identity cards and a camera.

On the night of the 24th March 1944, the prisoners prepared to escape through Harry, a tunnel measuring over 300ft long, beneath Hut 104.

Only 76 were able to escape before the guards spotted them and raised the alarm. Of those that got away, three made a 'home-run', 73 were recaptured and of those, 50 were shot while 'trying to escape'.

Camp commandant Colonel Von Luger informs Group Cpt. Ramsey that: "50 of your officers were shot while escaping".

Group Captain Ramsey: *Shot?*

How many of them were wounded?

Colonel Von Luger: *Here are the names of the dead.*

Group Captain Ramsey: *How many of the 50 were wounded?*

Colonel Von Luger: *None!*

The higher authority only directs me to inform you th... that 50 men were...

Group Captain Ramsey: (pause) *I see.*

The film ends with the caption "This picture is dedicated to the fifty".

In the film Group Capt. Ramsey points out to Roger that no matter how unsatisfactory this camp may be, *the High Command has still left us in the hands of the Luftwaffe. Not the Gestapo and the SS.*

To which Roger replies with stoic resignation: *Look, sir, you talk about the High Command and the Luftwaffe, and then you talk about the Gestapo and the SS. To me, they're the same! We're fighting the bloody lot! There's only one way to put it, sir: they are the common enemies of everyone who believes in freedom. If the High Command didn't approve of Hitler, then why didn't they throw him out? I've thought of the humiliation if we just tamely submit; knuckle under and crawl. Surely, you don't advocate that, do you, sir?"*

These men and many more like them fought and died for freedom and democracy, to free continental Europe from German occupation and Nazi oppression.

Today we have a European Union with an 'undemocratic' elite in control. Our politicians have connived on this state of affairs. Our free democratic sovereign nation is in danger of being destroyed by stealth. Our people were deceived into believing that the EU was just about trade, whereas in reality, it is about being drawn into a new undemocratic empire. All that is necessary now is to repeal the European Communities Act of 1972, withdraw from the EU and stop all financial (£55m/day and rising) contributions immediately. Or as UKIP prefer, activate Article 50 of the Lisbon Treaty, which provides for a sensible orderly exit over two years. We can then seek to rebuild our nation, seeing that it is composed of British people and only those immigrants who can reasonably be recognised as British.

Physical changes in Slough

Slough has been my home town since 1951 and has evolved nicely over a hundred years, where the old and new architecture blended in quite well. That was until the early 1960's when 'regeneration' got underway. This continued alongside the 'softly softly' mentality that became entrenched during the rest of that decade and beyond.

There appears to have been no attempt by Slough borough council to control subsequent development to recognise or complement the intrinsic qualities of the Town. There plan was to strip Slough of its history and heritage and rebuild it from scratch. The result has been that we have been swamped by a deluge of conflicting complaining architecture. Whole streets, passages and interesting nooks and crannies, that make a town interesting and appealing, have disappeared under concrete. Numerous hotels and coaching inns were in abundance along the High Street (London to Bath – A4) in fact the town was built up around them. The many pubs that were found on every corner have been replaced by office blocks, car parks and superstores. The imposing Tesco's superstore now occupies every last inch of the Licensed Victuallers School and its large gardens; the Sainsbury superstore, a half a mile along, in the same road, likewise, occupies the site where the Greyhound Stadium/Slough Town football club once stood. This to me, all ads up to a complete planning disaster, more than that though; sheer incompetence is a more fitting description.

Council leader at the time, Denis James must bear the greatest responsibility for the changing face of Slough. Town planning 'commander' James came under heavy criticism for allowing developers carte blanche to carry on with their own weird and wonderful creations, oblivious to what was already around them. Under his watch, the town was becoming a cluttered heap of architectural eccentricities where adjacent developments were permitted to clash alarmingly, lacking any kind of sympathy for their immediate surroundings, and often dwarfing other developments of merit. I am not against sympathetic redevelopment if it were to include the preservation of some of Slough's grander buildings in order to retain some of our local history. William Herschel's house for example and the Central Methodist Hall; The Leopold institute and the General Post Office were fine examples. The Congregational Church, Church Street and The Rectory, Chalvey Park, the redevelopment of the 'green triangle' site, and the demolition of 'Brookside House' and gardens, in Salt Hill are to name but a few. All are now under concrete.

What I find particularly sad is the destruction of the part of the town that is now the town square, which once was Chandos Street. Named after the Marquis of Chandos (afterward 2nd Duke of Buckingham).

This was just a narrow side street but contained more shops than most villages do. My favourite was the Pet shop, affectionately called Slough's Little Zoo.

Starting at the top of the street adjoining Wellington Street from North to South were two very attractive semi-detached Victorian (Villa's) houses, then a group of terraced cottages with very long front gardens. Next, was the corrugated iron Slough Labour Memorial Hall, frequently used by the MP's Benn Wolfe Levy, and then Fenner Brockway. There was an entrance to a car park which also had access from the High Street next to Ashley Russels the Ladies clothes store. Then there was John Perrings Furniture Store, This changed hands again and was taken over by Denham Motors as a car showroom selling Volkswagen cars. The shops that followed were Wadlows/Fishers Butchers, Dennis Harding Fishmongers, and the very popular Kum Wah Chinese Restaurant which relocated to the Windsor Road after its demolition. Next door was Gordon Burgess Hairdressers, then Stennings Boot and Shoe Repairs which subsequently became a Travel Bureau. Just before the pet shop was one of Sloughs many second-hand shops which was then taken over by Eric Stow as a Cycle shop. This short side street in which the Slough Billiard Hall was located also had so many distinctive shops that it was almost a mini High Street on its own. Grace Tobacconist had a shop in this street, as did Fletcher's Medical Supplies and also, G. Francis, Tailors. The very last shop on the east side corner of Chandos Street/High Street was 'Rabbitt' ironmongers. These were the family traders who had the house that I lived in, built, in 1888.

Directly opposite on the west side of Chandos Street was the General Post Office which was built around the same time, and handled all the outgoing mail. Outside, stood approximately half a dozen bright, gleaming red, telephone boxes. Next were the 'mews' (a courtyard containing buildings originally used as stables) in which stood a line of

BSA Bantam motorcycles, also painted in bright, gleaming red, with 'GPO' emblazoning on their leg shields in gold letters. These despatch bikes were used by uniformed young boys in pillbox hats, then later they were changed for crash helmets, to deliver telegrams as soon as they were received.

Next along, was Elliman's Embrocation factory and finally, at the top, on the corner with Wellington Street was the Drill Hall, built by James Elliman for the Volunteer Corps. James Elliman was a major benefactor, bringing huge changes to the town. His generosity also provided Slough with the Leopold Institute and Public Hall, the Fire Station and Salt Hill Playing Fields plus a substantial endowment fund for its' upkeep. Slough became a vibrant and successful town because of the compassion and benevolence of its fine businessmen, entrepreneurs and intellects.

During my research, I came across Reg Harrison's unique and fascinating set of 20 bound annotated volumes of photographs, newspaper clippings, written history, and over 700 slides showing how Slough has changed over the last hundred years.

He had the foresight to record this information before it was lost, and, as such, the collection contains material which cannot be found anywhere else. The collection has become one of the key parts of Slough's heritage. Reg joined his father's business, Harrison Cycle Co Ltd, in 1925 and worked in their first Slough Branch which opened that year and was a stalwart of the local community. He sadly died in December 1999.

In 2006 Reg Harrison's daughters kindly donated the entire collection to Slough Library so that the town could have permanent access to his collection.

The major 'facelift' which began in the 1950's then continued into the 1960's, overseen by the Labour party and masterminded by the notorious John King, was later taken over by the dictocratic, Councillor Denis James who single-handedly controlled the planning and redevelopment of Slough from 1983. With his iron grip on the planning committee, he was intent on securing maximum office development, with little or no discussion on the merits of any design submitted by potential developers.

There can be no doubt that Councillor James' resolute policy of generating his own office block boom has left its mark and created a monster. His view though was, 'don't be surprised if, in years to come someone doesn't try to put a preservation order on some of the buildings which are now being criticised'.

In all my life, I've never seen Slough in a worse state. The so called regeneration project has been going on for years and years and years, and all it has resulted in is utter chaos. Just take a look at Windsor Road for example: 'We just want our road to look nice' is what frustrated homeowners are saying.

In an attempt to totally erase Slough's history, the town-planners have, step by step, bulldozed huge swathes of our Victorian town and swamped it with a deluge of complaining architecture, all too often, at the expense of good taste. This office expansion has done nothing to improve the fortunes of our town, as too many remain empty.

In their quest to bring economic, social and environmental benefits to Slough, the councils four-lane carriageway 'Gate-way to Slough' project is trying to bring prosperity to Slough at any cost. This is sheer folly! All they will bring is more traffic, more congestion and a town virtually unnavigable for its residents.

Just take a look at the new road layout in Wellington Street, Tesco's and the Bus station for a glimpse into the future. This is where the 'gateway' from all directions will converge. Add to this, the Heathrow expansion and the increased air traffic, flying at rooftop level, right above your head; and to quote the late John Betjemen, Slough really 'won't be fit for humans'. The saga continues...

Summing up

Okay, the war had brought this country to its knees and millions of lives had been sacrificed to free Europe from tyranny but, still, we had an ordered society steeped in history. We had maintained the 'Rule of Law', 'Magna Carta' '*Habeas Corpus*' and our own 'Bill of Rights' but it had cost us dearly. In fact, we only paid off our war debt to America in 2006.

We were though, a free and victorious nation but faced the enormous task of rebuilding our battered country.

The whole point of my story is to show that, although we were poor, and things were hard for my mum, bringing up seven children on her own without the support of my dad! The system in place was good; and although it wasn't easy, we survived with the help of kind and honest people. What's more, there was plenty of opportunity to work hard and get on. We had a good foundation and things could only improve. Couldn't they?

Many people ponder the meaning of life; does God exist? Etc, etc. and can sometimes get a bit hung up with it all. So here's my take on it: we aren't born evil but are influenced by our surroundings and the people we associate with. We have our own free will to do as we please and our conscience to guide us. I also, sort of go along with Nigel Farage in his book *Fighting Bull* when he says: "I am a Christian in the normal English way - I love communing with my ancestors who built the mighty English church and who lie in its churchyard… I approve of Jesus. He seems a decent sort who liked his wine and the company of riff-raff, knew when to pick up the whip and set about him and displayed exemplary manners with that girl caught enjoying a little light relief. Seriously though, try not to be too serious".

Your family, friends and neighbours were with you from the beginning; from the day you were born, and are all the people in the world that you need. Those that you encounter, admire, aspire to be like, or simply just connect with, exist throughout your life or psyche, and I believe, affect your emotions, and behaviour, either consciously or sub-consciously. So you develop according to your life's experiences. People often say: 'you bring out the best in me', 'that person is a bad influence on you', or 'mix with your own kind'. At the end of the day, God gave us all our own free will. So a good rule of thumb is, let your conscience be your guide.

Recently I met up with someone that I hadn't seen for 40 years, we began talking about that time long ago and gradually remembered all the names of people we had known, that had since moved on, or of friends who had tragically died young, and together, concluded that times had changed, and that it's not like that now and not likely to be ever again in our life time. How many times have you heard it said: 'that was an end of an era'? Ultimately, it's all part of your era. Fortunately, I was born at the end of one era and grew up at the beginning of a new one. My era is what I have attempted to impart to you in the preceding pages of this book. My hope is to show you, particularly the younger readers, that we are a great nation and what we are living through now is not how it has to be. We are not, presently, a self-governing independent nation because of our continued subservience (membership) to the European Union which makes too many of our laws, but things are beginning to change at long last. Nigel Farage once described the European Union as a a Lego construct, forced together by an impatient child regardless of the shapes and colours of the pieces. Its components strain against one another before it has even been completed and must one day fall. Like the Soviet Union it will surely fall. In many ways they are almost identical monsters in that the non-elected, nominated each other into key positions and cannot be called to account. The people were told that the creation of one nation was imperative and that all nationalities and customs must be abandoned.

The town of Slough that I grew up in was as good a place, if not better than any other to work and live. Everything was within walking distance. You knew or were familiar with everyone in the town i.e. if strangers arrived they were noticed even in this large working town. All shopping was done locally in specialised friendly shops who delivered locally. Socially, this gave rise to a strong and cohesive society which combined safety and accessibility with a Bobbie on every corner.

Compare this today with, online shopping, out of town shopping centres and a huge array of 'Take-away's'; the traffic, the massive road networks and everyone in a hurry, all this adding nothing to improve the health of the nation, to a time when you went everywhere on foot or by public transport. There was no stress!

I grew up with people much like myself, but now when I go to town, I feel like the outsider and rarely see anyone I know, or hear English being spoken. The factories on the Trading Estate and the farms up and down the country, used to bustle with activity producing things, including our food, that were used and needed by us, right here on the door step. Now all, probably, imported from around the world; the consequence of that, being a lack of jobs.

There was discipline in the schools, street and houses and a community that was mutually helpful. There was a visual presence everywhere from, the park keeper and the road sweeper, to the delivery vehicles and the housing inspectors; and an effective judicial system.

Nowadays, people go everywhere by car and rarely leave them. I began to see the transition when Doctor Beeching cut many British rail lines to the bone, because the government of the day believed that a national road network system would become a modern replacement and the preferred mode of transport to the antiquated 'Iron Horse'. This gave rise to increased car ownership, congestion and the building of bypasses in almost every town up and down the country. The M25 has been the country's largest 'car park' since its inception with a never ending road widening plan, and consequently, this dire situation has forced many back onto the, hopelessly inadequate, railway. Another thing that hasn't helped was the decision to move freight from the railway onto the road.

Change is inevitable and we must progress. Because of the decline in passengers, the bus service deteriorated in and around Slough. It wasn't uncommon for bus services to be missed out or cancelled altogether and quite often for two or three buses to turn up empty and in convoy at the same time. On more than one occasion after waiting an age for bus, they'd sail past, not bothering to stop at all. It was diabolical. To cut costs, the one-man-operated was introduced, completely changing the atmosphere and behaviour on board. Passengers were being attacked and killed on the buses. So bad is it now that the driver has to remain in his cab behind a protective screen. That is the sort of progress we can do without.

Of course the Combi-boiler has replaced the coal fire, and a great improvement to home comfort it has become, but we can have both can't we? I have.

The point I'm trying to make is: why abandon a tried and tested model, for something 'new and trendy'?

If it ain't broke, don't try to fix it!

Memories are a golden chain.

The 2015 General election result was disappointing for UKIP but a good result for the country, giving Cameron his first all-Tory Cabinet. Confidence and stability too, was restored to the markets. A hung parliament could have meant weeks or months of political wrangling and parliamentary chaos in an attempt to cobble together a majority government.

Then with just a few days to go before the most important election in a generation the Labour leader ED Miliband indulged in the most foolish of stunts when he made the laughable decision to have his party manifesto carved onto an 8ft stone, only to be mocked by his opponents, likening him to the Old Testament prophet Moses, who received the Ten Commandments on a tablet of stone.

The SNP had played a massive part in this election and the electorate were terrified at the prospect of Red Ed planting his tombstone in the garden of number 10 and being forced to dance around it while the Scots Nationalists and the Union power barons took turns to call the tune.

Milibands Labour result was sealed when during the BBC leaders debate, SNP leader Nicola Sturgeon, dictated to him that he would do a deal with the SNP in order to keep a Tory government out of number 10.

As he sought to distance himself from the SNP during that heated exchange he appeared weak, and with no help from the audience, was outclassed by the emboldened Nicola Sturgeon. It was clear that the SNP sought to use Labour as a springboard to gain more power.

The SNP have nothing but contempt for anyone who doesn't agree with them and appear to ignore the British respect for free-speech and reasoned debate. Screams of 'traitor', 'Judas' and 'warmongering scum' directed at Scottish Labour leader Jim Murphy were totally futile and a waste of breath.

The hostility of some of them was evident in the run-up to the referendum on Scottish independence and was becoming more aggressive.

Miliband then went on to show a complete lack of judgement with a clandestine night visit to Russell Brands East London flat, broadcast on youtube, which was branded a 'joke' and blasted as a 'loony leftie love-in'. Milibands team no doubt thought this stunt would appeal to younger voters.

Despite all the poll predictions, the only real poll that matters, as they say, is the one taken on election night. This was the people's victory alright and it was won in middle England, not in Scotland. Sadly amongst all the hype, UKIP failed to cause an earthquake, in terms of seats won. Losing one of their only two MP's and failing to get Farage elected. This isn't the end for UKIP though, far from it as can be seen from the reslts below. If Cameron drags his feet there will be more defections; and by-elections.

Conservative votes won 11,334,576 - 36.9% = 331 MP's
Labour votes won 9,347,304 - 30.4% = 232 MP's
UKIP votes won 3,881,099 - 12.8% = 1 MP

If instead of 'first past the post' voting system a 'proportional representation' voting system had been used. The Conservatives would have obtained 224 MP's, Labour 208 MP's and UKIP 80 MP's.

David Cameron now has a perfect opportunity to take on Brussels, but the question is whether he will be tough or clever enough to take advantage of of it. Also, his honeymoon isn't going to last long, so he must get started straight away on all the sensible and important things that for decades Middle England has craved for: such as a reduction of the Quangos and regulations, addressing the human rights laws, boundary reform, curb immigration and axe the fixed-term parliament while the other parties are in disarray.

The real battle ahead, though, in the run up to the EU referendum will be that against the deceitful propaganda from the 'In Campaign' directed at the British public, similar to the warning that failure to join the single currency (euro) would have disastrous consequences for the UK. That turned out to be a huge lie.

Cameron is committed to an in/out referendum by the end of 2017, but he will have to find unanimity among 27 EU leaders and that will be a tough nut to crack. However, he is 'confident' of success saying, "I am going to get on with the job, get my head down for these discussions and deliver". Speaking at a summit in Latvia in 2015, he stressed his mandate for reform, saying that the British public were not happy with the UK's current relationship with the EU and that they would have the final say on whether to remain a member.